The Case for the Green New Deal

The Case for the Green New Deal

Ann Pettifor

VERSO
London • New York

First published by Verso 2019
© Ann Pettifor 2019

The moral rights of the author have been asserted

1 3 5 7 9 10 8 6 4 2

Verso
UK: 6 Meard Street, London W1F 0EG
US: 20 Jay Street, Suite 1010, Brooklyn, NY 11201
versobooks.com

Verso is the imprint of New Left Books

ISBN-13: 978-1-78873-815-6
ISBN-13: 978-1-78873-827-9 (UK EBK)
ISBN-13: 978-1-78873-828-6 (US EBK)

British Library Cataloguing in Publication Data
A catalogue record for this book is available from the British Library

Library of Congress Cataloging-in-Publication Data
A catalog record for this book is available from the Library of Congress

Typeset in Fournier MT by Hewer Text UK Ltd, Edinburgh
Printed and bound by CPI Group (UK) Ltd, Croydon CR0 4YY

I dedicate this book to my school-striking grandsons: Django and Theodore Pettifor-Carey.

The law locks up the man or woman
Who steals the goose from off the common
But leaves the greater villain loose
Who steals the common from off the goose.

The law demands that we atone
When we take things we do not own
But leaves the lords and ladies fine
Who take things that are yours and mine.

The poor and wretched don't escape
If they conspire the law to break;
This must be so but they endure
Those who conspire to make the law.

The law locks up the man or woman
Who steals the goose from off the common
And geese will still a common lack
Till they go and steal it back.

Anonymous (seventeenth century)

Contents

Preface

We can afford what we can do. This is the theme of the book in your hands. There are limits to what we can do – notably ecological limits, but thanks to the public good that is the monetary system, we can, within human and ecological limits, afford what we can do.

For humanity to survive on a liveable planet there is an urgency to what we must, and can, do. We are facing extinction. The earth's complex life support systems of atmosphere, oceans, land surface and life forms are at the point of breakdown, according to the world's top scientists. As George Monbiot has warned, 'Only one of the many life support systems on which we depend – soils, aquifers, rainfall, ice, the pattern of winds and currents, pollinators, biological abundance and diversity – need fail for everything to slide.'[1]

The UN's Intergovernmental Panel on Climate Change (IPCC) issued a clear and trenchant call for action in 2018. We need to cut annual global emissions by half in the next twelve years and hit net zero carbon by the middle of the century. According to Jason Hickel in *Foreign Policy* magazine,

> It would be difficult to overstate how dramatic this trajectory is. It requires nothing less than a total and rapid reversal of our present direction as a civilization. The challenge is staggering in its scale, and the stakes are even more so. As the co-chair of an IPCC working group put it, 'The next few years are probably the most important in our history.' After decades of delay, this is our last chance to get it right.[2]

For the UK and US, as well as other OECD countries, averting climate breakdown means cutting CO_2 emissions by 80 per cent by 2030 and reaching a zero carbon economy by 2040. This will allow OECD emission cuts to be equitably shared with non-OECD countries' emission cuts (as in the 1992 UN Convention on Climate Change's 'common but differentiated responsibilities' (CBDR), in which OECD nations have to cut first and hardest).

To protect earth's life support systems and to achieve such a radical transformation we must escape from capitalism's globalised, carbon-belching financial system – designed and engineered to issue trillions of dollars of unregulated credit to fund supposedly limitless consumption, and in turn to furiously fuel toxic emissions. It is an economic system that over a relatively short period of human history has wrecked earth's natural systems. And thanks to capitalism's dependence on a system enriched by imperialism, racism and sexism, it has bound all human societies to a form of slavery.[3] And yet, some have made historically unprecedented capital gains from this system. They are the '1%'.

As the *Economist* noted back in 2012, the wealthiest 1 per cent of Americans not only get more of the pie; they are increasingly creatures of finance. Steve Kaplan and Joshua Rauh of Northwestern University reported that investment bankers, corporate lawyers, hedge-fund and private-equity managers have displaced corporate executives at the top of the income ladder. In 2009 the richest twenty-five hedge-fund investors earned more than $25 billion, roughly six times as much as all the chief executives of companies in the S&P 500 stock index combined.[4] And yet the financial system on which these wealthy individuals have gorged is not itself a private asset. It is instead a great public asset, financed, guaranteed and sustained by millions of ordinary taxpayers in all the economies of the world. In other words, a great public good has been captured by the 1 per cent. It needs to be restored to collective ownership.

At the same time, environmentalists have treated the ecosystem for too long as almost independent of the dominant economic system based on deregulated, globalised finance. Macroeconomics, monetary theory in particular, are deemed a subject for 'experts' – the 'creatures of finance' that control the globalised financial system. Much of what is done within that system is deliberately kept hidden from society's gaze. Even so, many continue to avert their gaze from the activities of the finance sector, partly because the system appears too complex and remote, but also because we all benefit from it in some way. Millennials and pensioners alike enjoy the freedom that globalised finance provides for those who wish and can afford to travel widely among foreign lands and cultures. Many appreciate the ease with which bank accounts can be accessed in remote places, along with the ability to purchase and transport goods from anywhere on earth by making a bank transfer with just the click of a computer button.

I will argue that we can no longer afford to indulge such freedoms and powers, or to bend to the will of the gods of finance. There will be no chance of protecting earth's life support systems if we do not simultaneously escape from the grip of the masters of the globalised financial system. A capitalist system that is blind to the most vital capital of all: that provided by nature, which finds itself exploited parasitically and used up at a reckless rate, as E. F Schumacher argued in his 1973 classic, *Small Is Beautiful*.[5]

By escaping from the inexorable control of the masters of the financial universe, we will find that we can afford to create a new, more balanced system of international economic and ecological justice. That we can also afford to reforest large swathes of the earth and its coastal areas. We will discover that we can afford to urgently end the globalised economy's addiction to fossil fuels. That we can afford to transform our economy away from its fixation with 'growth'. That we can, within our own finite physical and intellectual limits, begin to restore our damaged ecosystems to health. That we can work together, collectively, to protect ourselves, our families and communities and the environments in which we survive, grow, develop and create.

In other words, we can – and to survive, we must – transform and even end within the next ten years the failed system of capitalism that now threatens to collapse earth's life support systems and with them, human civilisation. We must replace that economic system with one that respects boundaries and limits; one that nurtures 'soils, aquifers, rainfall, ice, the pattern of winds and currents, pollinators, biological abundance and diversity';[6] one that delivers social and economic justice.

We Green New Dealers know we can achieve that in the ten years or so that the UN's scientists believe are left to us. One reason it is achievable is this important fact: just 10 per cent of the global population are responsible for around 50 per cent of total emissions. Tackling the consumption and aviation habits of just 10 per cent of the global population should help drive down 50 per cent of total emissions in a very short time. This understanding helps us grasp the rate and scope of what is possible if we genuinely believe climate breakdown threatens human civilisation.[7]

Furthermore, we know we can do this because we have, in the past, undertaken huge transformations within less time than that suggested by the 2018 IPCC Report. Our confidence should stem not only from knowledge of past transformations, but also from a new understanding of money and monetary systems. I am determined to ensure that this knowledge is shared, in order to empower campaigners and environmentalists with economic evidence and arguments with which to confidently challenge purveyors of capitalist economic dogma, the climate deniers, defeatists and naysayers. Those who consider it utopian to believe society can end a deeply entrenched system of racialised capitalism. Those who are convinced that 'there is no money' for transformation, and that government spending is inflationary. Those who feel that capitalism's hyper-globalisation is working just fine. That poverty, racial and gender inequality and injustice are not a result of globalised capitalism, but rather of human weakness. That decent jobs for all is a pipe dream. That humanity has survived previous periods of climate breakdown – and will do so again. That humanity is essentially evil and driven by greed and self-interest. That there is no hope.

Not true. There is hope; and it rests not on a utopian vision of humanity, but on our knowledge of human genius, empathy, ingenuity, collaboration, integrity and courage. We know that it is possible to transform the globalised financial system because we have done it before – and in the relatively recent past. That too will be a theme of this book.

To transform the current economic and financial system we must ignore defeatists on both the left and right of the political spectrum, and arm ourselves with sound knowledge. Such knowledge can empower millions of people, and be a motor for action.

Above all, it will serve to correct widespread and deliberate misinformation about the workings of the great public good that is the monetary system. Falsehoods peddled by the followers of Hayek and Ayn Rand; by mainstream economists, cryptocurrency fanatics and other monetary 'reformers', and all those who either passively or actively defend a financialised capitalist economy that deliberately depletes the earth's finite and precious resources.

In a fine speech in 1962, President John Kennedy boldly announced,

> We choose to go to the moon in this decade and do the other
> things, not because they are easy, but because they are hard,
> because that goal will serve to organise and measure the best
> of our energies and skills, because that challenge is one that
> we are willing to accept, one we are unwilling to postpone,
> and one which we intend to win, and the others, too.

'We choose to go to the moon.' In 1962 there were serious doubts as to whether the world's scientists and engineers possessed the intellectual and physical resources, and astronauts the courage, to build and steer a spacecraft that might reach the moon. But there were absolutely no doubts, or questions, about the ability to finance a 'moonshot'. In the event, scientists from around the world collaborated on the project, one of the most ambitious international team efforts ever. Just seven years after Kennedy's speech, in 1969, Neil Armstrong stepped out of his spacecraft and onto the moon.

We can choose to survive. But in order to survive, everything must change. Everything. Radical action, based on sound understanding of the financial system and moral courage, can transform the present and guarantee a future.

> Sometimes we just simply have to find a way. The moment we decide to fulfil something, we can do anything. And I'm sure that the moment we start behaving as if we were in an emergency, we can avoid climate and ecological catastrophe. Humans are very adaptable: we can still fix this. But the opportunity to do so will not last for long. We must start today. We have no more excuses.[8]

INTRODUCTION
What Is the Green New Deal?

Origins

'A Green New Deal, with Justice for All. Practical. Possible. Inevitable.'

Those words formed the heading of a plain google doc that popped up on my screen in July 2018. They were to be the basis of a carefully crafted manifesto, tested with a range of Alexandria Ocasio-Cortez's (AOC's) friends and advisers as she prepared for the US mid-term Congressional elections. They helped her win a victory that was to electrify millions of young Americans and reinvigorate the youth wing of the Democratic Party.

Earlier that year members of the AOC campaign team had visited Britain to sound out a range of economists working with, and around, Jeremy Corbyn, and to prepare for Ms Cortez's upcoming Primary campaign. I met with one, Zack Exley, in a coffee shop to discuss the thorny question of financing their ambitious plans. After that, apart from the odd email, I heard no more. Hardly surprising, as the New York Primary campaign was in full swing and, by all accounts, absorbed much energy. Plus, there was considerable doubt whether AOC could successfully challenge a powerful and well-funded sitting Democrat. In the event, she pulled off a stunning victory.

The day after that victory the think tank where I work, Policy Research in Macroeconomics (PRIME), was contacted again by her team. We agreed to convene a small, trusted group of British economists in my apartment to deepen and broaden the discussion of how to finance AOC's programme. We had a lot in common, including a shared commitment to the Green New Deal (GND).

Ten years earlier, a group of British environmentalists and economists had spent many evenings in that same apartment, sustained by comfort food and the odd glass of wine, while furiously arguing, strategising and drafting a plan for transforming the economy to protect the ecosystem – a plan we called the Green New Deal. Our meetings began in the summer of 2007 and continued through the height of the 2008 Great Financial Crisis. These events, the fall of Lehman Brothers, the debates on quantitative easing (QE) and bailing out the banks, injected a grave sense of urgency into our deliberations.

While we were early adopters in 2008, we were not the

first to call for a GND. That call had been made on 19 January 2007 by Thomas L. Friedman, a *New York Times* journalist in a column titled 'A Warning from the Garden'.[1] 'The right rallying call is for a "Green New Deal",' Friedman wrote. 'The New Deal was not built on a magic bullet, but on a broad range of programs and industrial projects to revitalize America . . . If we are to turn the tide on climate change and end our oil addiction, we need more of everything: solar, wind, hydro, ethanol, biodiesel, clean coal and nuclear power – and conservation.' The call was taken up first by President Obama, who included the Green New Deal in his platform.

Later, in the autumn of 2007, Colin Hines, a onetime British Greenpeace staffer and campaigner, took up Friedman's challenge and convened a group to draft an ambitious plan for a Green New Deal that might both transform the economy and safeguard the planet. Besides myself, the group included Britain's only Green MP, Caroline Lucas; the macroeconomist and senior trade union economist, Dr Geoff Tily;[2] the *Guardian*'s economics editor, Larry Elliott; the environmental campaigner and author, Andrew Simms; Jeremy Leggett, director of an international solar solutions company, Solarcentury; the tax and accounting expert, Richard Murphy; and two recent directors of Friends of the Earth, Charles Secrett and Tony Juniper.

Our report, published in July 2008, called for 'joined-up policies to solve the triple crunch of the credit crisis, climate change and high oil prices'. It argued that the global economy is facing . . . a combination of a credit-fuelled financial crisis, accelerating climate change and soaring energy prices underpinned by an encroaching peak in oil production. These three overlapping events threaten to develop into a perfect storm, the like of which has not been seen since the Great Depression. To help prevent this from happening we are proposing a Green New Deal.

July 2008 was a strange time, a hiatus between that bleak day in August 2007 – when inter-bank lending froze and liquidity in capital markets evaporated – and the collapse of Lehman Brothers in September 2008. Central bankers had rushed to provide liquidity to investment banks in August 2007 when their bankruptcy threatened global systemic failure. The publicly financed and taxpayer-guaranteed bailouts of that month appeared to work. Regulators and politicians were lulled into believing the crisis had been managed.

The American and British public appeared to accept this view. By July 2008, people were going about their daily lives reassured that the worst had been averted, unaware that a huge global investment bank was about to implode and blow up the global financial system. It was during this strange lull in the crisis – *a crisis that as I write, is still not over* – that we tried to gain political traction for the Green New Deal.

Initially, the United Nations Environment Programme (UNEP) took up the call because of the GND's 'enormous economic, social and environmental benefits . . . ranging from new green jobs in clean tech and clean energy businesses up to ones in sustainable agriculture and conservation-based enterprises'.[3] In 2009, Gordon Brown called for an international 'green new deal' to boost the environmental sector and help lift the global economy out of recession, while Green members of the European Parliament called for a European Green New Deal to tackle the continent's economic problems in a sustainable manner. Despite this support, both in Europe and the United States (where the Green Party took up the call) our efforts were soon eclipsed by the chaotic aftermath of the Lehman Brothers bankruptcy.

Ten years later, Alexandria Ocasio-Cortez and her team came up with their own, ambitious Green New Deal – a 'plan to solve three critical problems at once: the threat climate change poses to America's security, poverty and inequality, and the racial wealth gap'. Central to the US GND is the Job Guarantee, to give 'every unemployed American who wants one, a job building energy-efficient infrastructure'.

This is how a young woman of colour, the youngest person ever elected to the US Congress, ignited a political torch under a radical proposal for preventing the collapse of earth's life support systems. Her plan went viral on 13 November 2018, when young people blocked the corridors of US Congressional power with the warning that climate breakdown threatened their futures. The Sunrise Movement corralled the newly elected Democrat into joining their sit-in outside the office of Nancy Pelosi, likely next Speaker of the House of Representatives. Together they demanded political backing for a Green New Deal.

At the time of writing, that political backing has not been forthcoming. Indeed, climate breakdown did not make it into the 2019 Democrat leadership's list of priorities for the new Congress. Speaker Pelosi was dismissive, despite claiming on her Congressional website that she had 'made the climate crisis her flagship issue'. Instead, she went on to disparage the Green New Deal as 'one of several or maybe many suggestions that we receive. The green dream, or whatever they call it, nobody knows what it is, but they're for it, right?'[4]

Yet a survey conducted by the Yale Program on Climate Communication in December 2018 found that the AOC's Green New Deal had 'strong bipartisan support'. Most Democrats and 64 per cent of Republicans backed the plan, without knowing it was promoted by a Democrat.[5] Millennials (those aged between eighteen and thirty-seven) supported the Green New Deal by nearly a thirty-point margin, according to a poll conducted by the *Nation*.[6] Evidence of its potential popularity did not prove sufficient to persuade the Democrat leadership, older American voters, mainstream Democrats or right-wing Republicans.

This worrying lack of support for a sound and rational programme for tackling climate breakdown and economic injustice was the spur that drove me to write this book. For, as the environmental journalist David Roberts argues, while there is immense potential energy in the GND, '*converting that heat to power* – to real results on the ground – will involve a great deal of political and policy engineering, almost all of which lies ahead.'[7] If we are to convert that heat to power, supporters of a Green New Deal must explain how policy can be engineered so that their visionary programme can be financed – without transferring the burden of higher taxes on to the working class (often defined in the US as the 'middle class').

At the heart of the scepticism around the GND lie these questions: how, realistically, can such a radical transformation be brought about within ten years or so? How can today's governments and their allies in the private sector afford to finance such a transformation? What will happen to workers in fossil fuel industries? This book will attempt to address those questions.

But first things first.

What Is the Green New Deal?

The Green New Deal demands major system change: both economic and ecological system change. It demands structural (governmental and inter-governmental) changes, not just behavioural, community or technological change, in our approach to the financialised, globalised economy and ecosystem. In addition, and as in the 1930s, such change must be driven by a radical structural transformation of the economy, particularly the financial sector.

The idea was developed in Britain in 2008 on the understanding that finance, the economy and the ecosystem are all tightly bound together. Protecting and restoring the ecosystem to balance cannot be undertaken effectively, we argued, without the transformation of the other sectors. Joined-up policies are needed. Financing the hugely costly overhaul of the economy away from its dependence on fossil fuels cannot be achieved without the subordination of the finance sector to the interests of society and the planet.

Environmental advocates tend to focus on individual ('change your lightbulbs') or community ('recycle, reuse, reduce, localise') action. We have been slow at understanding and promoting the need for radical systemic change across sectors and at a global and national level; that is, change that involves state action. And such structural change cannot just be undertaken at the level of international agreements on carbon budgets.

Its ambition is on a far grander scale than Roosevelt's 1930s New Deal (even if his administration also faced an ecological catastrophe: the Dust Bowl). The climate threats we face are of a magnitude beyond the imagination of New Dealers. However, we can learn from Roosevelt's administration. To tackle climate change we need simultaneously to tackle the root cause of growing toxic emissions: a self-regulating, globalised financial system that pours exponential quantities of unregulated credit into the hands of speculators and consumers. This credit is used in turn to inflate the prices of existing assets, while failing to finance the creation of new tangible and intangible assets. Further, it is used to accelerate the extraction and consumption of the earth's finite assets. Only once we switch off the 'tap' of 'easy money' will it be possible to switch off the flow of oil and other fossil fuels.

These joined-up policies lie at the heart of the Green New Deal.

The demand for a Green New Deal is realistic in that it harks back to an era when the global economy was transformed almost overnight by the revolutionary Keynesian monetary policies of an American president. As Roosevelt began dismantling the globalised 'gold standard' on the night of his inauguration, on 4 March 1933, he freed up his administration to end austerity and unemployment, then running at 25 per cent, before deploying fiscal policy to create jobs and transform the domestic economy, but also to address the Dust Bowl crisis. He affirmed, as Keynes had done, that 'we can afford what we can do.' Because the financial system – as a system – exists to enable us to do what we can do, no more and no less. As then, now it must be returned to its role as the servant, not the master, of the economy and ecosystem.

The Green New Deal is, therefore, a plan. It is not an idea, nor a proposal, but a comprehensive *plan* for stemming the breakdown of earth's life support systems. It is comprehensive in that its drafters understand that the earth, in all its diversity, needs a 'new deal', and so do the men, women and children who – in all their diversity – are the victims of ongoing global economic failure, and, now, of climate breakdown.

The GND recognises that in the future we must derive energy only from renewable sources. We also need to expand and support ecosystems that suck huge amounts of carbon dioxide out of the air and store that carbon in trees, soils and oceans. But societies also need to end their dependence on a globalised economic system that drives climate breakdown and encourages toxic emissions; an economic system that leads to ecological imbalances alongside economic, political and social inequality and injustice. Its name is globalised, financialised capitalism.

While there is widespread agreement on these essential elements of both the US and British Green New Deals, there are also differences.

The US Green New Deal (2018)

The US Green New Deal is ambitious. It is presented in impressive detail in the Resolution submitted to the US Congress by Rep. Alexandria Ocasio-Cortez, Democrat-N.Y., and Sen. Ed Markey, Democrat-Mass., on 5 February 2019.[9] It is a comprehensive plan for achieving five major goals in the course of 'a ten-year mobilisation':

- to reach net-zero greenhouse gas emissions through a fair and just transition for all communities and workers;
- to create millions of good, high-wage jobs, and ensure prosperity and economic security for all people of the United States;
- to invest in the infrastructure and industry of the United States to sustainably meet the challenges of the twenty-first century;
- to secure clean air and water, climate and community resilience, healthy food, access to nature, and a sustainable environment for all;
- to promote justice and equity by stopping current, preventing future, and repairing the historic oppression of frontline and vulnerable communities.

The Resolution begins by acknowledging that 'whereas the Federal Government-led mobilizations during World War II and the New Deal created the greatest middle class that the United States has ever seen . . . many members of frontline and vulnerable communities were excluded from many of the economic and societal benefits of those mobilizations'.

The Job Guarantee

The Resolution goes on to recognize 'that a new national, social, industrial, and economic mobilization on a scale not seen since World War II and the New Deal is a historic opportunity to (1) create millions of good, high-wage jobs in the United States; (2) to provide unprecedented levels of prosperity and economic security for all people of the United States; and (3) to counteract systemic injustices.'

A key assumption within the Resolution is that the state will provide and leverage 'adequate capital . . . including through community grants, public banks, and other public financing . . . for communities, organizations, Federal, State, and local government agencies, and businesses working on the Green New Deal mobilization'. The formulation is deliberately vague.

Research and policy development for the US Green New Deal is undertaken by scholars at the nonprofit think tank, 'New Consensus'. Demond Drummer and Rhiana Gunn-Wright are leading the policy work including the proposal for the creation of a 'green bank'. In an interview, they explained that this public bank 'would be used to invest in zero-carbon technologies under development in the public and private sector that need to be commercialized. The bank would be designed to offer financial enhancements and support to communities that haven't had access to clean energy and transportation.'[10] But that is just the beginning. 'Right now we're focused on what needs to be done and how all the pieces fit together,' Drummer explained in the same interview. 'Then we will focus on how to pay for it. To be clear: It's a question of how we will pay for it – not if we can afford to pay for it. America can afford what we decide to do.'

The UK Green New Deal (2008)

The British Green New Deal had a quite different orientation from the American version.[11] While the American GND is heavily focused on the domestic economy, the British version, written at the height of a globally contagious financial crisis, adopted a more internationalist perspective. We began by locating the breakdown of earth's life support systems in the current model of financial globalisation, and argued that 'a positive course of action can pull the world back from economic and environmental meltdown.'

We were ambitious, too. We wanted to combine stabilisation in the short term with longer-term restructuring of financial, taxation and energy systems of the global economy. We urged the UK to take action at the international level to help build the orderly, well-regulated and supportive policy and financial environment required to restore economic stability and nurture environmental sustainability.

'Financial deregulation' had in our view 'facilitated the creation of almost limitless credit. With this credit boom have come irresponsible and often fraudulent patterns of lending, creating inflated bubbles in assets such as property, and *powering environmentally unsustainable consumption.*' We were also clear that high, real rates of interest had driven the need for excessive rates of return on investment necessary to repay costly debt. Hence the compulsion to strip the forests, empty the seas and exploit labour in order to generate the returns needed to repay debts.

Our report therefore began with proposals for systemic change to the global economic model as an essential precondition for decelerating climate change. We understood that global transformation was necessary if we were to re-regulate the *domestic* financial system to ensure the creation of money at low rates of interest consistent with democratic aims, financial stability, social justice and environmental sustainability.

Fundamental to the British GND is the understanding that over the centuries advanced societies have developed monetary systems. The concept of money and a system of money evolved to enable us 'to do what we can do' (Keynes). Money is and always was a form of social technology, one that enables individuals, firms and governments to do business, to trade and exchange. To accomplish transactions smoothly and efficiently, both at home and across borders. A society's monetary system, like its sanitation system, we argued, is a great *public* good.

However, we also recognised that the history of monetary systems is one of struggle for control over the system, between those that would exercise *private authority* over it and those that prefer *public, accountable authority*. In the 1960s and 70s, Western governments ceded effective control over the system to a private authority – 'the market'. Or, to be more specific, private actors in financial markets. The latter are dominated by the capital bourses of Wall Street, the City of London and Frankfurt.

While a developed monetary system is a great public good, we Green New Dealers recognised that there are of course ecological, economic and political limitations to what society can 'do' within the framework of the monetary system. Nevertheless, provided they are managed by the visible hand of public authority, monetary systems could help finance the radical and costly transition from a fossil fuel-based economy to one based on renewable energy. Just as the monetary system helped finance transitions to war, or to recovery from financial crises.

Therefore the UK GND makes clear that one of the first tasks will be for society to regain *public authority* over the national and international monetary system. And next, to raise the finance to tackle climate change, not just in Britain but internationally. We called on the British government to support a transformation of the financial system that would:

- allow all nations far greater autonomy over domestic monetary policy (interest rates and money supply) and fiscal policy (government spending and taxation);

- set a formal international target for atmospheric greenhouse gas concentrations that keeps future temperature rises as far below 2°C as possible;
- deliver a fair and equitable international climate agreement to succeed the Kyoto Protocol in 2012;
- give poorer countries the opportunity to escape poverty without fuelling global warming by helping to finance massive investment in climate-change adaptation and renewable energy.

We drew our inspiration from Franklin D. Roosevelt's 'courageous programme' launched in the wake of the Great Crash of 1929. We called for a sustained programme to invest in and deploy energy conservation and renewable energies, coupled with effective demand management.

A Carbon Army to Make Every Building a Power Station

Like the US GND, we placed considerable emphasis on the creation and training of what we termed a 'carbon army' of workers to provide the human resources for a vast environmental reconstruction programme. The production and distribution of clean energy will demand the skills, professionalism and experience of many that currently work in an industry that must contract until it finally shuts down – the fossil fuel industry. We called for hundreds of thousands of these new high- and lower-skilled jobs to be created in the UK, regarding this as part of a wider shift from an economy narrowly focused on financial services and shopping to one that might become an engine of environmental transformation. We supported the Trade Union Congress's demand for strong policies to support workers through *a just transition* – one that will make sure that workers do not pay the price for the economy's transformation away from dependence on carbon and other greenhouse gas emissions.

Focusing first on the specific needs of the UK, we called on the British government to introduce a decentralised, low-carbon energy system that included making 'every building a power station'. Energy efficiency was to be maximised, as was the use of renewables to generate electricity. At the time we envisaged a £50 billion-plus per year crash programme to be implemented as widely and rapidly as possible. 'A programme of investment and a call to action as urgent and far-reaching as the US New Deal in the 1930s and the mobilisation for war in 1939'.

We argued for realistic fossil fuel prices that included the cost to the environment, high enough to create the economic incentive to drive efficiency and bring alternative fuels to market. We advocated rapidly rising carbon taxes and revenue from carbon trading. We called for the establishment of an Oil Legacy Fund, paid for by a windfall tax on the profits of oil and gas companies. We wanted the focus to be on smart investments that would not only finance the development of new, efficient energy infrastructure but also help reduce the demand for and the cost of energy, particularly among low-income groups, by improving home insulation.

GNDs: How Do They Differ?

Both the US and UK GNDs are based on the under-standing that because climate breakdown is a security threat to the nation as a whole, the state has a major role to play in the transformation – just as if the nation were facing the threat of war. The American Green New Deal is 'a Federal Government-led mobilization' work-ing alongside, and integrating, the private sector within GND programmes. In drafting the GND the Justice Democrats drew heavily on the work of Professor Mariana Mazzucato, whose research has shown that contrary to myth, public organizations have played a critical role as 'investor of first resort' in the history of technological change and advance. From the iPhone to Google Search, the world's most popular products were funded, she concludes, not by private companies but by the taxpayer.[12]

The British GND also has a major role for the state, not just in the transformation of the energy sector, but also the finance sector – and at international as well as domestic levels.

While the British GND is concerned to protect low-income individuals and families during the process of transformation, the AOC GND is more ambitious. In the words of the veteran climate campaigner Bill McKibben, it seeks to 'remake not just a broken planet, but a broken society'.[13] It puts members of 'frontline and vulnerable communities' front and centre as beneficiaries of the Green New Deal. The drafters of the Resolution are acutely conscious of the 1930s New Deal's 'intimate partnership with those in the South who preached white supremacy',[14] and of the deliberate and racist exclusion of many black people from the economic gains of that era. Hence

> it is the duty of the Federal Government to create a Green New Deal ... to promote justice and equity by stopping current, preventing future, and repairing historic oppression of indigenous communities, communities of color, migrant communities, deindustrialized communities, depopulated rural communities, the poor, low-income workers, women, the elderly, the unhoused, people with disabilities, and youth (referred to in this resolution as 'frontline and vulnerable communities').

The British Green New Deal, as noted above, has adopted a more internationalist perspective than the American versions of the programme, calling on OECD governments to help finance massive investment in climate-change adaptation and clean energy for low-income countries.

Finally, the British Green New Deal (in both the first and subsequent reports) provides something absent from the US version in that it expands on the question of how the GND could be financed, deploying both monetary and fiscal policy, but with an emphasis on monetary policy.

1
System Change, Not Climate Change

We have been warned by climate scientists that to avoid the most dangerous impacts of climate breakdown and global heating, then humanity collectively has (starting from 1870) a 'carbon budget' of about 3,200 billion tonnes of carbon dioxide emissions to work with.[1] At the current rate of global emissions, this budget would be used up within ten to twelve years. Worse, in 2019 another group of scientists, the UN's Intergovernmental Science-Policy Platform on Biodiversity and Ecosystem Services (IPBES), warned that nature is declining globally at rates unprecedented in human history. The rate of species extinction is accelerating, with grave and immediate impacts on people around the world.[2] The UN called for 'a fundamental, system-wide reorganization across technological, economic and social factors, including paradigms, goals and values'.[3]

The Green New Deal (GND) is a blueprint for bringing about that urgent system-wide reorganization within a short time period.

The first question we should ask is, whose deal is this? Can the Green New Deal be a single global plan, implemented by a global authority, or can it be managed more locally?

As Herman Daly, pioneer of ecological economics and the architect of 'steady state' economics, has argued: the human economy is a subsystem sustained and contained by a delicately balanced *global* ecosphere, which in turn is fuelled by finite flows of solar energy.[4] The earth's life support systems do not recognise boundaries. So can the New Deal work on any lesser scale than the totality of the globe?

While the impacts of the current crisis are felt everywhere, the largest share of historical and current global emissions of greenhouse gases originated in rich countries. Meanwhile, per capita emissions in poor countries are still relatively low. Ecological justice therefore requires a major redistribution of wealth, from rich producers and emitters of toxic fossil-fuel emissions, to low-income countries.

Furthermore, as the Global Commons Institute (GCI) has argued, rich countries must reduce emissions until per capita emissions converge across the world. The proposal for 'contraction and convergence' has for some time now been advocated at the UN.[5] It has failed to gain traction because global institutions are weak, are largely unaccountable and lack political leadership. It is clear we cannot rely on global initiatives as the only hope.

There is an alternative approach: international cooperation based not on global institutions, but on the authority of nation states. For the Green New Deal to be transformational, its implementation must be at the level of democratic accountability. Policies agreed at an international level would be implemented and enforced by locally and nationally accountable institutions that reflect domestic conditions.

But even if we can create policy at the level of the state or of local government, does this mean that those active in the markets of the global financial system will support the policies of different nation states? Will the existing dollarized financial system – no longer tethered to the real economy – support and finance a Green New Deal at national level? We have to get real and accept that, with some exceptions, the sector would not help finance a massive climate stabilisation project on terms that are acceptable and sustainable.

As things stand, those that operate in globalised capital markets behave as 'masters of the universe'. They remain aloof and unaccountable to the governments and communities for whom the transformation of systems is an urgent task. If we are to mobilise the financial resources needed for the massive changes required to conserve, restore and sustain life on earth, then the globalised financial system must be subordinated to the needs of nations, and made servant to the task of transformation.

If the global sector is to be tamed, then a first challenge will be to tackle the hegemony of the currency that sustains globalised finance: the United States dollar.

Imperial Power and the US Dollar

The pre-eminence of the dollar came about as a result of the US strong-arming the rest of the world into adopting its currency as the world's 'money' at the 1944 Bretton Woods conference. Keynes had argued for a global currency, not tied to any one country, and managed in the interests of the international community. He was defeated at Bretton Woods, as the US imposed its will on a weakened Europe. Today that decision still allows the US to enjoy a 'free lunch' at the expense of the rest of the world. Its 'exorbitant privilege' is a reward for the insurance it provides the rest of the world, especially in times of crisis. As the Federal Reserve acts as global lender of last resort, the US made trillions of dollars available to European and Asian banks during the Great Financial Crisis of 2007–9. This 'insurance' is valuable at times of crisis, but it could just as easily have been provided by an independent, international central bank working with, and answerable to, all nations, not just the most powerful.

The 'exorbitant privilege' enjoyed by the United States is remarkable given that the country sustains ever-rising external debt and deficits, because global demand for the dollar exceeds US production.[6] In contrast to Britain's imperialist role as a *major exporter* of capital, the US is a major *capital importer*. It uses its power to attract financial resources, surpluses of capital from Asia and the oil-exporting countries.

A second great benefit the United States enjoys is the power to borrow in its own currency, over whose value it has some control. This means that the US avoids the exchange rate risks faced by other countries when they borrow and have to repay in a different currency. If the dollar were to depreciate, that would not matter to US authorities, as the nation does not own debt issued in euros, yen or sterling. When the dollar falls in value, the debts owed by the United States fall in value too. Thus the dollar as the world's reserve currency regularly affords the US cheap, low-risk finance with which to sustain its large trade deficit and its exorbitant consumption of the world's goods and services.

The hegemony of the dollar in global finance remains unchallenged despite the recent financial crisis, as the historian Adam Tooze has pointed out. In fact, the US dollar did not merely survive the 2008 crisis, but was reinforced by it.[7] As a result of both the global financial crisis and the weakness of the Obama administration, Wall Street banks are bigger and more powerful than before the crisis. That outcome was not inevitable. It was largely due to a failure of progressive, global leadership by the Obama administration. Unlike Roosevelt, Obama had no direct experience of Wall Street and its ability to inflict systemic economic failure on millions of innocent Americans and their families. Instead his advisers, such as Alan Greenspan, Larry Summers and Robert Rubin, were themselves architects of the globalised and deregulated financial system. Under the Clinton administration they had teamed up to defeat a plan by Brooksley Born, the chair of a federal agency, for stronger regulation of derivatives. In 1999 Summers and Rubin together pushed through the repeal of the Roosevelt administration's 1933 Glass–Steagall Act, which had prevented banks backed by taxpayer guarantees from being affiliated with investment banks that engaged in financial speculation.

The Obama administration's support for Wall Street has been compounded by the Trump administration, dedicated to upholding and weaponising Wall Street power. To fortify its imperial overreach, the US budgeted $750 billion (3 to 4 per cent of US GDP) for defence in 2020, and stoked talk of further foreign invasions – what the US presidential candidate Bernie Sanders calls the 'forever wars'.

Fuelling Consumption, Inciting Corruption

Backed by a great imperial power, the US dollar works hand in hand with 'the invisible hand' of the market – or, less abstractly, with the invisible hands of powerful agents active in financial markets. It is a globalised system committed to 'the constant expansion of production and driven by the constant impetus to capital accumulation', to quote Simon Pirani of the Oxford Institute for Energy Studies.[8] It is a system that, enabled by the dollar's power to breach regulatory barriers, has deliberately been detached from democratic oversight at the level of nation states. Its purpose is to accumulate wealth for the tiny minority that operate in the finance sector. This is achieved through the production of, and speculation in, intangible financial assets, most notably credit.

Credit is the main driver of economic expansion (defined by economists as 'growth') and consumption. It has stimulated the extraction of fossil fuels through industrialisation, urbanisation, motorisation and the growth of mass material consumption and consumerism by the affluent classes, in both high- and low-income countries.[9]

Deregulated credit in a world of mobile capital does not just fuel consumption, it also incites corruption, of both the political and finance sectors. Drug dealers, traffickers and gangsters engaged in a global trade responsible for roughly 450,000 deaths as a result of drug use in 2015, which has made them among the wealthiest beneficiaries of today's system of unregulated, globalised, mobile capital.[10]

Credit is presumed to 'grow' exponentially as private finance enhances capitalism's ability to, first, create society's new 'wants', what J. K. Galbraith called our 'psychologically

grounded' desires: 'wants' that do not 'originate in the person-
ality of the consumer', but are 'contrived by the process of
production'.[11]

In this way, the spigot of easy credit denominated in
dollars fuels global economic expansion and the constant
impetus to capital accumulation by the already-rich.
Consumption gorges in turn on fossil-fuel extraction,
accelerating the growth of greenhouse gas emissions
(GHGs).

From the perspective of the ecosystem, perhaps the most
damaging aspect of globalised, largely deregulated credit-
creation is the finance sector's demand for high, real rates
of return on a relatively effortless process: the creation of
new money. If interest rates are higher than the capacity of
the earth, or the economy, to renew itself, then interest
rates become brutally extractive. People who are obliged
by low or falling incomes to borrow are driven to work
ever-longer hours to raise the money needed to repay the
interest on their debt. Firms, too, cut costs and exploit
labour more intensively in order to raise the finance needed
to service their debts. Governments strip the forests, trawl
the seas and exhaust the land to improve 'efficiency' and
generate the returns needed to repay their obligations,
including foreign debt service.

Bring Offshore Capital Onshore

It is my view – expanded in the next chapter – that to manage economic expansion, halt the impetus to capital accumulation and lower GHGs, it is essential to first manage the spigot of globalised credit creation. To that end, it will be necessary *to bring offshore capital back onshore*, and to subject the system to accountable management and regulation at the level of the state. Next, to manage the global crisis of earth systems breakdown we will need an international currency independent of the sovereign power of any single, imperial state. Finally, we will need to establish an international 'clearing union' for the settlement of credits and debits between nations as we go about sharing the burden of transformation.

Many will regard such proposals for radical global system change as utopian. And so they will be – until a global shock makes system change inevitable.

The plain fact is that societies have over time developed monetary systems that make the mobilisation of financial resources eminently possible for society's urgent needs. Given the establishment of these systems, there need never be a shortage of money. But publicly backed monetary systems cannot be managed and deployed in the interests of society and the ecosystem as long as they remain 'globalised'– captured and moved offshore, beyond the reach of regulatory democracy. In what is effectively the financial stratosphere, monetary systems serve the interests not of societies but of the global 1%. This has not happened by accident. As the result of a deliberate process, the financial system has been detached from the real economy of nation states and from governmental regulation. Following the logic of neoliberal economics, it has been 'encased' to protect the sector from democratic interference, as Quinn Slobodian shows in his book *The Globalists*. In other words, globalised, dollarized financial capitalism shifted offshore has undermined the power of democratic governments and local communities to develop economic policies to meet urgent needs.

We have been here before. Today's globalised system harks back to the gold standard system of the 1930s when the private finance sector wrested control of publicly backed monetary systems away from democratic governments. At the time those that argued for 'system change' – the dismantling of the gold standard – were thought delusional. When the system did collapse, many economists were shaken to the core. Mistakenly, they had believed the gold standard was, like gold, immutable.

We Must Take Back Power

Given the vast power of dollarized globalisation over the world's economies, can governments as rich as Germany's or as poor as Mozambique's mobilise the finance needed for the transition to a liveable planet? Could governments cooperate to mobilise the finance needed by the world's poorest countries? We know there are ample financial resources (savings) to pay for the transition. But do societies and their governments have the power to realise these resources?

The straightforward answer is no. That fact presents Green New Dealers with the first grand mission: nothing less than global financial system change. If we are to support the campaigning efforts of Extinction Rebellion and the school strikes movement; if we are to fulfil the goal of a fundamental, system-wide transformation of the economy to save the ecosystem, then we must combine and cooperate at an international level to bring about a revolution in the power relations of the globalised and dollarized economic system.

As I explain below, cooperation and coordination between a progressive British economist and an American president and his administration brought about such transformation in 1933 and again, less successfully, at Bretton Woods in 1944. We can do so once more – equipped with sound economic theory and political practice to mobilise our collectively paralysed societies. The purpose will be to transform the globalised financial system within which the domestic economic systems of nation states are situated and integrated, and to which they are subordinated.

Given these challenges, and given today's politics, the task of transforming the system may seem insurmountable. But, as David Roberts wrote in 2019: 'We are not in an era of normal politics. There is no precedent for the climate crisis, its dangers or its opportunities. Above all, it calls for courage and fresh thinking.'[12]

Before we explore what must be done, we must first tell the correct story of how we got here. That is difficult because, as Rana Foroohar argues, 'financialisation is the least studied and least explored reason behind our inability to create a shared prosperity.'[13]

So, how *did* the financial system globalise, and what can we learn from that?

2

Winning the Struggle with Finance

Thanks to globalisation, policy decisions in the US have been largely replaced by global market forces. National security aside, it hardly makes any difference who will be the next president. The world is governed by market forces.

Alan Greenspan, former chair of the Federal Reserve

Today our financial system is governed by private, not public, authority, a fact which lies at the heart of our current global malaise. In the West, we have recently seen yet another period of global debt inflation yoked to deflationary austerity policies. The current rise in indebtedness exceeds that which predated the global financial crisis of 2007–9, and it may well lead to another catastrophic debt deflation. The impotence of elected governments in the face of declining living standards has led to the rise of plutocracies, intolerant 'populism', and racism, fuelled by extreme and entrenched levels of inequality both within and between countries. Some observers point to parallels with events in the 1930s and to the rise of German fascism. Is that fair? Can history help make sense of our present world? Yes, if we understand recent history as a contest between democratic societies and the private finance sector for control over banking systems and the economy. To grasp the nature of this struggle we could start with the political economist Karl Polanyi, who in 1940 explained that 'in order to understand German fascism, we must revert to Ricardian England'.[1] Then as now, to understand today's global insurgencies we should revert to Ricardian England.

David Ricardo (1772–1823) was a financial speculator as well as an economist with a marked interest in distribution and class conflicts. He was an advocate of free trade, the quantity theory of money, hard money, the law of comparative advantage and other principles of classical economics.[2] His theories led Britain to establish a 'gold standard' in 1821 by which sterling was valued in relation to the gold or bullion stored in the vaults of the Bank of England. This system sought to ensure that Britain's foreign financial assets (including debts) could be valued, fixed and repaid in terms of gold rather than in currencies whose value fluctuated. Britain was then the world's largest trading nation, with London at the centre of world commodity markets. The City of London was the world's dominant and imperialist creditor and, like the US today, issued the world's reserve currency.

The international gold exchange standard, as the system was called, became the fantastic machinery of global financial self-regulation – designed to operate beyond the control of governments.[3] Under the standard, governments were pressured by the private finance sector to uphold the 'rules of the game'. Cross-border movements of both capital and trade had to be deregulated, driven by the invisible hand of market forces, not managed in the interests of the domestic economy. Nations that built up imbalances or deficits were penalised by capital flight and outflows of gold that would deflate economic activity, lower prices, increase unemployment and encourage bankruptcies. The reverse would happen, too. Nations that earned more abroad would benefit from inflows of gold and the automatic inflation of the money supply.

The City of London's creditors favoured the system because loans to foreign governments and corporations were redeemed not in their domestic currencies but in the British empire's currency (sterling), whose value was fixed in relation to gold. Debt repayments were not to be eroded by inflation or devalued by volatile currencies. The system prioritised private financial interests over the interests of nation states, and limited the ability of governments to adopt policies that protected their economies. Pressure was applied on governments by international creditors to re-orient their economies towards revenue-raising exports.

The hard currency raised was used to repay international creditors. (The IMF insists on much the same today when it imposes 'structural adjustment' programmes on debtor nations and forces poor countries to prioritise foreign debt repayments.) Export sectors that generated revenues and earned 'hard' currency (sterling), took precedence in the economy over domestic economic activity.

The gold standard evolved into a system that obliged governments to turn to, and rely on, international capital markets – that is, private wealth – for finance. Governments and their central banks were 'discouraged' from adjusting exchange rates, interest rates and fiscal policy to favour the domestic economy. Instead these important economic levers were subject to the whim of actors in capital markets.

The system was based on distrust of the state by owners of private wealth. There was particular distrust of the ability of democratic governments to manage the economy, to tax or impose tariffs and to address domestic concerns. As Quinn Slobodian explains, 'it is wrong to see neoliberals as critics of the state per se but correct to see them as perennial skeptics of the *nation*-state.' In 1979, F. A. Hayek, the father of neoliberal economics, called for 'a true international law which would limit the powers of national governments to harm each other.' He described this as the 'dethronement of politics', writes Slobodian, 'but it is just as obviously the dethronement of the nation. Just as proponents of militant democracy perceived a need to constrain democracy, proponents of militant globalism perceived a need to constrain nation-states and set limits on their exercise of sovereignty.'[4]

The EU as a 'Gold Standard' Region

The subjugation of sovereign debtor nations to the policies of the IMF, like the subjugation of European governments to the eurozone (EZ) system, provide a guide to what 'gold standard' economic powerlessness means. The economic ideology that informed EZ Treaties held that financial markets must be 'free' to operate beyond the reach ('intervention') of any European state. The theory dictates that financial markets be 'encased' and protected from regulatory democracy.[5] As Charles Goodhart, the distinguished monetary expert, explained in advance of the construction of the eurozone, the EU participating nation states would find 'their status . . . changed to a *subsidiary* level, in the sense that they can no longer . . . call upon the monetary authority to create money to finance their domestic national debt. There is to be an unprecedented divorce between the main monetary and fiscal authorities.'[6]

The European currency – the euro – is structured to eliminate the lender of last resort function for the central banks of member states, without creating such a function at European level. Without the support of their own central bank, eurozone states are obliged to turn to private, globalised capital markets for finance. At the same time the rigid 'rules of the game' embedded in EU Treaties effectively strip European governments of economic agency. In my view it is that lack of agency that is the cause of economic failure and social and political instability within the eurozone. Countries like Greece, Italy and even France or Germany lack the power to adjust their economies to suit domestic markets, conditions and interests. This economic helplessness enrages the public and has led to the rise of what is euphemistically known as 'populism'.

The plain truth is that Greece, Italy and France are not alone. Europe is not unique in its subordination to the private authority of globalised, dollarized financial markets. All democratic states are powerless in the face of a global monetary system 'governed' by private market forces. This is highly relevant to the Green New Deal. Why? Because mobile agents active in globalised, deregulated financial markets have very little interest in supporting states that need to wean economies away from dependence on fossil fuels and from the all-powerful corporations that dig up, distribute and make money from those fuels.

The gold standard did not last. Its collapse proved Polanyi right when he affirmed that a self-regulating and autonomous economic sphere is a utopia.[7] Today's dollarized globalisation is equally utopian. The question we face is this: will it, or can it, be transformed by progressive forces? And can that be done in time to finance the Green New Deal? The alternative is that it will collapse in a welter of crises reminiscent of those that led to the fall of the gold standard in the 1930s. So can the system be transformed in

a rational manner to regain public authority over economies – in order to deal with the threat of planetary collapse?

To answer that question, and to build confidence in the
possibility of transformation, the following is a brief review
of the history of recent failures and successes in winning
(and albeit then losing) the contest for control over the
international financial and monetary system.

1919: A Struggle for Public Authority over the Money System

We begin the story just a hundred years ago, at the Palace
of Versailles, outside Paris. It was there that the First World
War's victorious Allies met to negotiate the notorious
Peace Treaty of that year. John Maynard Keynes, at the
time a young member of the British delegation, played a
key role in the negotiations, as Eric Rauchway documents
in his book *The Money Makers* (2015). He paints a vivid
picture of the strikers that stormed the streets of Paris on
May Day, 1919, on behalf of the revolutionary ideals of
that time. Keynes and other diplomats dodged rioters and
strikers, and after the fighting stopped had to step over, or
around, the bodies en route to the Palace of Versailles.

While the streets of Paris were chaotic, defeated
Germany was in turmoil. The humiliation of the armistice
had led to a naval uprising, to the forced abdication of the
German Kaiser, and to the election of revolutionary coun-
cils. By then, too, the Bolsheviks were firmly entrenched in

Russia. Keynes was well aware of the dangers posed to civilisation at this pivotal moment in economic history. To prevent further bloodshed and violence, and to block the emergence of Bolshevik-style governments in Europe, it was necessary, he believed, to resolve debts and to restore employment, incomes and economic stability.

He set about producing a simple, but nevertheless revolutionary, plan for the rehabilitation of Europe and the reconstruction of the international financial system. It was developed effectively on the back of an envelope. The plan was checked and amended as he deepened his understanding of German and Allied economies' assets and liabilities. Central to his plan was his conception of money as a social construct, based on trust. For Keynes, it was the responsibility of public, not private monetary institutions to underpin and enforce society's trust in money.

The problem he addressed was this: the Germans owed the British money, but had no capacity to pay, nor the capital to invest in reconstruction of those assets that would generate income for the repayment of debts. The British owed the Americans money, but they too had no capacity to pay – unless the Germans paid.

The solution he devised can be briefly summarised as follows: Germany would issue what was then the enormous sum of £1 billion in bonds. These were nothing more, in the words of Joseph Schumpeter, than 'promises to pay'. The bonds were to be backed and guaranteed, Keynes proposed, by Allied governments; effectively by the millions of taxpayers that backed the public institutions of Allied countries. Investors that bought German bonds would obtain an asset (the interest-bearing bond). As the asset was backed by the largest economies in the world, it would be safe. Its safety rendered it valuable collateral, to be used to leverage additional finance. So much for the benefits to creditors. For the debtor, Germany, the finance raised by the issue of the bonds would enable the prostrate Reich to pay most of what it owed the Allies in reparations and debt, and to finance the reconstruction of the German economy.

There were terms and conditions, of course. Few politicians trusted their defeated enemy, especially the humiliated German military. So the rate on the bond was high, 4 per cent, while 70 per cent of the value of the bond was to go to pay reparations to the victors. Only the remaining 30 per cent would be used for Germany's reconstruction. Participating nations would guarantee the bonds jointly and severally. And the League of Nations would impose penalties or foreclosure if Germany defaulted on her debts.

Keynes was ambitious. The bonds would do more than help Germany recover; they would also be acceptable as payment between Allied governments and as first-class collateral at central banks. In other words, they could act as a form of intergovernmental currency or 'money' – backed not by gold, but by the economic strength and taxpayers of the Allied nations. He aimed not only to restore economic stability to the warring parties, but also to establish a sound international framework within which nation states could collaborate and begin to revive employment and other forms of economic activity at home.

In this sense, Keynes's plan was revolutionary. It was the first step in the abandonment of a system of money backed by a finite commodity, gold, and managed by *private authority*. Instead the money raised by the German bonds was backed by the economies and taxpayers of the Allies, and would be managed by *public authority*. It replaced a system governed by the private authority of financial markets with one governed by the public authority of states.

Keynes's ambitions went further: he hoped that in the future the Allied-backed bonds would form the basis of a new international financial architecture based on an independent reserve currency, one managed by an international 'clearing bank'.

Under his 1919 scheme, the Germans could use the bonds as collateral to raise more finance for debt repayment and reconstruction. The French could use the bonds to pay debts to the British, and the British to pay debts to the Americans. The plan included provisions for other Central Powers and new nations to issue similar bonds, also secured by richer government allies. In other words, the bonds would become a new form of international currency – to pay for international transactions.

The key point of Keynes's 'Scheme for the Rehabilitation of European Credit and for Financing Relief and Reconstruction' was this: it redesigned and reconceptualised the world's economic and financial architecture. It proposed a new international financial order based not on gold bars and private financiers, but on economic strength and the autonomy of states. It was a plan that permitted Germany's economy to be restored to stability and prosperity within a sound and very necessary *international framework*. Keynes's plan saw states and their governments playing a pivotal role in providing finance for recovery, employment and regeneration across Europe – and doing so within an international and cooperative framework in which no nation was dominant.

He sent his proposal to the British Treasury and to the prime minister, David Lloyd George. They enthusiastically backed the scheme and put it to their allies, including President Woodrow Wilson of the United States. But Wilson rejected the proposal out of hand. His letter was forthright: the risk was that the Americans, having the most robust economy, might be left 'holding the bag'.

Keynes agreed that this could be the case, but America could afford to bear the cost of worldwide recovery. After all, the US had incurred no foreign debts to finance the war. Second, Americans had profited immensely from the conflict, thanks not only to Wall Street's financing of the belligerents, but also from increased munitions exports to warring Europeans. Furthermore, if the American economy was to remain buoyant, then it was vital for American goods to find export markets in Europe – and for those exports to be financed.

Unbeknown to Keynes, and only recently revealed by Rauchway, Wilson's letter of rejection was not by his own hand. Instead it was drafted (why is anyone surprised?) by Wilson's adviser, the chief executive of J. P. Morgan, Thomas W. Lamont.[8] Lamont, via Wilson, indicated that he preferred to see Wall Street provide the finance for recovery. When Wilson wrote about 'the desirability of post-war lending going through the usual private channels', it was the voice of 'the usual private channels' behind his letter.[9] Acting in the interests of his class, Lamont objected to any proposal that prioritised Allied-backed 'bonds [meaning government bonds] over all other obligations', meaning private bank bonds. His bank, J. P. Morgan, had expanded its foreign lending to governments during the First World War and could not risk repayment being deferred, or *subordinated* to publicly backed bonds.

The consequences of American opposition to Keynes's scheme were catastrophic, and, as the years passed, must have caused him great personal as well as professional anguish. Thanks to Wall Street lobbying, and to Mr Lamont's closeness to the presidency, the fantastic free market machinery of the gold standard was restored in the United States in 1920 and in Britain in 1924. This was followed, predictably, by bouts of credit inflation and debt deflation. As a result, the 1920s and 1930s witnessed a major financial crisis, mass unemployment and industrial unrest. The austerity imposed on the British economy to prepare for restoration of the gold standard in 1924 led to the General Strike of 1926.

The United States too suffered from the failure to adopt Keynes's plan. Post-war industrial production peaked in January 1920 and then (in part because of the collapse in trade) the economy moved into a major depression, with production levels dropping by 32.5 per cent in March 1921. After the 1920–21 bust, Wall Street's laissez-faire bankers churned out credit and financed the 'Roaring Twenties' boom. This led to the massive inflation of debt and was followed, again predictably, by a catastrophic *debt deflation*, the Crash of 1929 and the Great Depression. In Europe, foreign debts, economic instability, unemployment, deflation and austerity led to the rise of fascism, and culminated in the Second World War.

There were further consequences. Monetary hegemony passed to the United States. Central banks were made independent of political authority. Capital markets were liberalized. High, real rates of interest prevailed. And the UK was burdened by a colossal and crippling War Loan of £2 billion, issued at 5 per cent.

Thankfully the agony was alleviated in Britain in 1931. Labour Prime Minister Ramsay MacDonald had formed a minority National Unity Government in 1931 to defend both austerity and the gold standard, but soon had no choice but to abandon the 'cross of gold'. Then, in 1933, on the first night of his inauguration, President Roosevelt deliberately and systematically began dismantling the American, and then the global, gold standard.

In the 1930s both Britain and the United States, led by President Roosevelt's New Deal, turned away from a system based on *private* financial authority, which led to austerity, deflation and the threat of nationalism and fascism. Instead they embraced Keynes's monetary system first outlined at Versailles in 1919, and based on *public authority*, policy autonomy and democracy – and full employment.

The struggle to wrench the public good that is the monetary system away from Wall Street and the City of London had been won. What happened next?

The Original 'New Deal' of 1932

The words that today resonate worldwide as 'The Green New Deal' were first formally uttered in July 1932 by president-elect Franklin D. Roosevelt. In a speech accepting the Democratic Party's nomination as its candidate, he ended with a rousing promise: 'I pledge you, I pledge myself, to a new deal for the American people.'

Apparently, he had attached no special significance to the phrase 'new deal'. The very next day an alert cartoonist plucked those words from the speech and – in today's parlance – the term went viral.[10] Whatever its origins, henceforth it was to be the hallmark of the Roosevelt economic programme, and to acquire a status that has been revered by progressives ever since.

By the time of Roosevelt's elevation to the presidency in 1933, Keynes was world-famous. His attack on the economic clauses of the 1919 Treaty of Versailles in his polemic of the same year, *The Economic Consequences of the Peace*, caused controversy worldwide. It was accessibly written and widely read, including by the man who was to become US president. Keynes's regular attacks on the international monetary system and the 'barbaric relic' that was the gold standard made him notorious among the financiers of Wall Street and the City of London, where the deflationary gold standard was revered and vigorously defended.

Roosevelt was governor of the state of New York when the Wall Street house of cards collapsed in the Great Crash of 1929. He watched as 5,000 American banks failed and an average of 100,000 jobs vanished each week: almost 25 per cent of the American workforce was unemployed by the end of Roosevelt's governorship in 1932.

He had kept abreast of economic developments – not just as the governor of New York State, but earlier as a student. Historian Eric Rauchway explains that although Roosevelt completed his Harvard degree in three years, he stayed on for a fourth year, studying history and economics in graduate school, at the recommendation of his professors. He took courses on American economic development, the economics of railroads and other corporations, and money and banking.[11] But he had an independent mind. 'I took economic courses in college,' he later said as president, 'and everything I was taught was wrong.'[12] That experience did not make Roosevelt a fiscal radical. It made him a monetary radical.

In his inaugural speech, Roosevelt pledged to expel the 'money changers' from the temple of American democracy: 'faced by failure of credit they had proposed only the lending of more money . . . They knew only the rules of self-seekers and had no vision and when there is no vision the people perish.'

He explained that his administration would adopt 'lines of attack', 'safeguards' against a return of the old order; that there would be strict supervision of all banking and credits and investments; an end to speculation with other people's money, and provision for an adequate but sound currency.

That very night (a Saturday) he began the process of taking the US off the gold standard, and by Monday morning, 6 March 1933, Roosevelt was well into the dismantling and transformation of the 'barbaric relic' that was the globalised financial system.

Roosevelt's New Deal is often hailed as 'Keynesian' with its emphasis on fiscal (tax) policy, government investment and spending. But, in this author's estimation, that is wrong and a deliberate misnomer, for two reasons. First, what was genuinely Keynesian and radical about Roosevelt's New Deal were his *monetary* policies. By ending the gold standard and revaluing the currency, his administration was freed from shackles imposed by Wall

Street over both the exchange rate and fiscal policy. His initiatives brought the Great Depression to an end and stabilised the deterioration of public finances instigated by the deflationary 'austerity' policies of President Hoover. Public spending growth under Roosevelt (ahead of the war) averaged 8 per cent of GDP a year through to 1939, and 14 per cent of GDP from 1934 to 1936. Under President Obama's Recovery Act of 2009, the same measure grew by only 3 per cent of GDP a year over the 2009–15 period.[13] The rise in both the public debt and deficit as a share of GDP was arrested because the economy recovered, jobs were created, and tax revenues rose.

By dismantling the gold standard, Roosevelt and his advisers challenged the arrogance of the finance sector. His administration subordinated 'global market forces' to the priorities of a democratically elected president. By suspending both the system and the neoclassical ideology of the gold standard, Roosevelt courageously freed up his administration to resolve the banking crisis and to address the needs of millions of unemployed and poor Americans. Backed by a landslide electoral victory and wealthy enough not to need the backing of financiers, he literally wrenched power away from Wall Street. His actions are often interpreted as 'fixing the banks', but he did more. By triggering an end to the gold standard, he transformed the international financial system. And it was that *international system change* that enabled him to 'fix the banks'. Above all, it enabled his administration to intervene in the economy, to stabilise the banking system, and the exchange rate, to create jobs, and to implement an industrial, agricultural and environmental strategy. Those strategies paved the way to restoring stability and economic security.

In contrast to today's leaders, Roosevelt had the political courage and the leadership skills to challenge Wall Street. He was then free to respond to the public anger caused by the deflationary aftermath of the 1929 Crash, when millions had lost their jobs, and farmers and small firms had been bankrupted, while the drought that lasted through the 1930s wrought havoc on the land itself.

Today's leaders – plutocratic or otherwise – lack political courage, have a dearth of leadership skills, and are deferential towards global financial interests. Because of their defence of the status quo, they are not free to respond to the public anger that is rooted in the Great Financial Crisis of 2007–9. On the contrary, almost without exception, they use their powers to uphold and consolidate the current globalised system.

Public Authority and Nature's New Deal

The New Deal has especial resonance for environmentalists because of its role in tackling the ecological crisis of its day: the Dust Bowl. Although President Roosevelt's programmes were flawed in many respects, nevertheless one programme was remarkably successful in restoring forests and arresting soil erosion.

As a wealthy patrician, Franklin D. Roosevelt cared about the trees on his family's estate in Albany, NY, for economic as well as conservation reasons.[14] While aware that a movement was growing for the *preservation* of nature, as advocated by John Muir, founder of the Sierra Club, Roosevelt preferred to argue for the *conservation* of nature and found, first as a senator and then as governor of New York, that conservation was politically popular. During his tenure as governor, according to Neil Maher: 'Just a few months after Black Tuesday (in 1929) Roosevelt asked the state legislature for an appropriation to fund a tree-planting program, similar to that initiated by the Boy Scouts, to provide jobs for New York's growing unemployed population.'[15]

This experience influenced the creation of the Civilian Conservation Corps (CCC) a month after Roosevelt's inauguration in 1933. James McEntee wrote the final report of the CCC in 1942, when Congress terminated the New Deal programme, and recorded that, remarkably, the Corps

> was responsible for planting more than 2 billion trees [now estimated at 3 billion], slowing soil erosion on 40 million acres of farmland, and developing 800 new state parks. It also constructed more than 10,000 small reservoirs, 46,000 vehicular bridges, 13,000 miles of hiking trails, and nearly 1

million miles of fence, while simultaneously stocking America's rivers with 1 million fish and eradicating almost 400,000 predatory animals from the nation's forests, farmlands and prairies.[16]

The CCC was responsible for over half the reforestation, public and private, done in the nation's history. It's estimated that nearly three million men – about 5 per cent of the total male population – took part in the CCC over the course of the agency's nine-year history.[17]

Because Southern Democrats were anxious about the threat to their racial order posed by Roosevelt's programmes, and because the president depended on their support, he bowed to their racist demands for the segregation of whites and blacks within the Civilian Conservation Corps. This remains a cause of deep resentment among African Americans. And the CCC was discriminatory in other ways. While the program enrolled (and segregated) some 200,000 young African American men[18] and 88,000 Native Americans living on Indian reservations, it excluded women completely – despite Eleanor Roosevelt's attempts to establish CCC camps for females. While Roosevelt considered male unemployment a civil problem to be corrected through federal programs like the Corps, he saw women laborers as less than workers and therefore not entitled to the same economic rights.[19]

Despite its deep flaws, the CCC of the 1930s helped to

democratise conservation, and also redefined it. The project triggered a national debate that expanded the meaning of conservation beyond the careful use of national resources, to include concern for human health, the need for ecological balance, and the importance of wilderness preservation promoted by thinkers such as Aldo Leopold. Its legacy resonates to this day.

Wall Street and the City of London Fight Back: The Bretton Woods Era

Britain and the United States began to prosper after the end of the gold standard system in 1933 and in the run-up to the Second World War. Yet, despite the obvious gains from the transformation, the struggle to regain private control over the system continued almost immediately after delegates returned from the 1944 Bretton Woods conference. Wall Street, aided by the City of London, did not give up.

The creation of the post–Second World War Bretton Woods financial system was an attempt by economists to reinforce the new Keynesian monetary system that had been put in place by the New Deal. In 1944 world leaders delegated their top economists (from the Global South as well as the North; from Britain and the US, but also from Russia, Africa and India[20]) to confer and then to build an international financial architecture – to be named the Bretton Woods system – that would continue to defend government sovereignty over economic policy.

The system designed by J. M. Keynes and others at Bretton Woods was not the one he had first dreamed up in 1919. It was imperfect, largely because the United States opposed the creation of an independent, international currency and a 'clearing union' for balancing surpluses and deficits between nations, and to maintain international economic stability. Instead, the US used its post-war dominance to insist on the dollar as the world's currency. Soon, even this imperfect system came under attack from Wall Street and the City of London.

In his book *Moneyland: Why Thieves and Crooks Now Rule the World and How to Take It Back*, Oliver Bullough relates the story of how the revolution in global finance was triggered by one bank in 1962. The dismantling of the Bretton Woods system, he explains, was down to the determination and ingenuity of a powerful London banker, Siegmund Warburg. A German outsider in the City of London, he was a man who 'lived for deals' and who wanted more than anything to restore private dominance over the finance sector. His bank, S. G. Warburg and Co., began the process of dismantling Bretton Woods by dealing in Eurodollars, and trading 'offshore' beyond the reach of US Regulators. The initial plan was to get hold of three billion US dollars holed up in secret Swiss bank accounts, package them up, and lend them on at a profitable rate of interest. However, his planned new bond issue hit a buffer:

the Bretton Woods system of checks and balances for the management of cross-border flows of capital.

If Warburg's bonds, which he intended to exchange for Swiss cash, had been issued in Britain, there would have been a 4 per cent tax on them. So the bank formally issued them at Schiphol airport in the Netherlands. If the interest were to be paid in Britain, it would have attracted another tax, so Warburg arranged for it to be paid in Luxembourg. His bank managed to persuade the London Stock Exchange to list the bonds, despite their not being issued or redeemed in Britain, and talked around the central banks of France, the Netherlands, Sweden, Denmark and Britain, all of whom were rightly concerned about the eurobonds' impact on currency controls (the 'walls' of the oil tanker that was Bretton Woods). The final trick was to pretend the borrower was Autostrade – the Italian state motorway company – when really it was IRI, an Italian state holding company. If IRI had been the borrower, it would have had to deduct tax at source, while Autostrade did not have to.

The cumulative impact of this game of 'jurisdictional Twister' was a 'eurobond' that paid Warburg's bank a high, real rate of interest, on which no tax of any kind was paid, and which could be turned back into cash anywhere. The 'walls' of the international financial fortress had been breached, and henceforth eurobonds were to become the battering ram that broke down the carefully constructed Bretton Woods international system of managed finance. Thanks to Warburg's ambitions, investors in capital markets had been 'liberated' from the oversight and management of regulatory democracy. 'This is the dark side of globalisation, and there is no positive case to be made for it, unless you are a thief or a thief's enabler' writes Bullough.

By gradually discrediting and tearing down the Bretton Woods architecture in the 1950s and 60s, the finance sector and its friends in governments and academia dismantled the international framework of what is universally known as 'the golden age' of economics. On one Sunday night in 1971 – and without consulting any of his allies or indeed any international institutions – President Nixon, in an event that came to be known as the 'Nixon Shock', unilaterally dismantled the international financial architecture so carefully constructed at Bretton Woods. He did so without putting any other system in its place. Once again the international finance sector was in control. In the absence of a sound international framework governed by public authority, societies and their elected representatives in both rich and poor countries were once again rendered relatively powerless. Democratic governments were denied effective agency over the management of domestic economies. By the 1960s, financial deregulation had restored private authority over both the international financial system and national economies.

Since then, nation states and their governments have gradually been stripped of the power to direct investment (both public and private), currency exchange rates and interest rates. Instead this power is vested in global, invisible and unaccountable investors and speculators in financial markets – who are free to move their capital across borders without effective hindrance, and regardless of their impact on a nation's currency or interest rates.

Alan Greenspan was right. The world is once again governed by markets.

Is it any wonder that voters in countries as far apart as Brazil and Turkey, Britain and the Philippines, Russia and the United States, have turned to 'strong men', allegedly to 'protect' them, their jobs, their homes and their children from out-of-control, globalised 'market forces'?

Public Authority over the Green New Deal?

Governments (with the possible exception of the United States) with a mandate to expand public investment on the scale required by the Green New Deal will inevitably encounter the opposition of financiers, bankers, speculators and investors. These will demand high real rates of interest on capital; and the implementation of 'fiscal rules' to limit public borrowing, spending and investment, even while they simultaneously build up monstrous mountains of *private* debt.

How could they be effective? This is how. They would first threaten, and then launch, a rapid, large-scale exodus of financial assets and capital from the country concerned. They could also choose to boycott the market for government bonds. The rapid outflow of mobile capital would cause the nation's currency to fall in value. In response, the central bank might have to raise its base rate and oblige interest rates across the spectrum of lending in the real economy to rise. While higher rates might – only might – staunch the outflow of financial assets, they inevitably hurt those active in the real economy. As explained earlier, high rates would demand the extraction of even more labour and ecosystem assets for the repayment of debts.

The reason for the exodus of capital would be straightforward: private financiers believe (wrongly) that public finance 'crowds out' private finance. Their aim is to wear down states and privatise *all* investment, especially risk-free investment backed by taxpayers and governments. (In this sense, many so-called free market capitalists are intensely risk-averse.)

One hundred years ago, in 1919, Europe lay in ruins after a disastrous conflict. Powerful politicians, economists and central bankers offered no hope to the millions of unemployed people starving and struggling to rebuild lives after the long and brutal war. It was made clear by the public authorities that *there was no money*. The war had consumed government finances and left the Allied nations heavily indebted to each other, but especially to the United States. Sounds familiar? The cry went out loud and clear: *there is no money* for the vital and costly task of recovery from war and the building of peace.

One man challenged that orthodoxy and developed an international plan that could have saved the world from the catastrophes of the 1930s. His legacy has conveniently been either forgotten or marginalised.

What Must Be Done?

These are times that call for the intellectual and political courage of giants like Keynes and Roosevelt. If we are to implement the Green New Deal, then today's political leaders will have to act just as courageously and scrupulously. They will have to dismantle and transform the current globalized financial system and its embedded ideology, to regain the powers and public authority needed to protect and repair the earth's life support systems.

The world can no longer afford the orthodox economic logic of financialised, globalised capitalism. To secure a future for this and future generations we must, as Vishwas Satgar writes, overcome 'the eco-cidal logic of capitalism [with] a democratic eco-socialist nation-building project'.[21]

The success of the long and effective campaign to deregulate the financial system means that any nation-building project will be fiercely resisted. Private financial firms have for decades now displaced governments in the financing of activities that used to be the domain of the public sector: water, transport, education, housing, environmental services and health. The finance sector has been so successful in marketising and monetising every sphere of collective activity, that there remains almost no private or public asset or activity that has not been commodified, 'priced' and marketised globally. Prices of essential services – including health and higher education – have been hiked beyond the reach of millions of people, so that today they are a major cause of the scourge of inequality.

If, in the interests of the ecosystem, we are to move economies away from fossil fuels, then societies and their governments need to regain control over these key sectors. Public oversight and investment in areas such as water, energy, housing and transport will be vital to manage usage in the interests of the ecosystem and of society as a whole, and to make services more sustainable and affordable.

But public spending is not the only economic policy important to the Green New Deal. The exchange rates of currencies, the creation of credit and the rate of interest on credit are important policy levers that will be central to the financing of the Green New Deal in every part of the world. As we discuss in the next chapter, it is important that these 'economic levers' are managed in the interests of society and the ecosystem.

The use of these levers for public purpose will be strongly resisted by globalised private equity firms, asset management funds, banks, pension funds, hedge funds, to name but a few. As things stand, they are powerful lobbyists and as a consequence roam the financial stratosphere largely unfettered by democratic regulation or taxation, and with financial fraud effectively decriminalised.[22] But there is a lacuna in that political space, a profound contradiction in their position that GND activists could exploit. In fact, despite their abhorrence of state-run institutions and preference for privatisation and deregulation, global financiers benefit richly from the taxpayer-backed *public* sector and in particular from the services and resources of central banks. That dependence on public resources provides politicians and activists with potential leverage.

Later, I will explore the power taxpayers and their elected representatives have over the private finance sector – a power that lies latent, not sufficiently exploited to bring pressure to bear on Wall Street and the City of London.

3

Global System Change

Avoiding climate breakdown will require cathedral thinking. We must lay the foundation while we may not know exactly how to build the ceiling.

Greta Thunberg, speech to British
Parliament, 23 April 2019

Many will point out that the global financial system is backed by the most heavily weaponised empire in all history – the United States – and by Wall Street, Frankfurt and the City of London. The forces behind the system, they will rightly observe, are far too powerful for reform, never mind transformation. And moreover those forces have strong, 'woman-in-the-street', *public* backing. As a result, many of the proposals outlined below risk being scoffed at, not only by those heavily invested in the system, but also by thoughtful readers, who will raise legitimate questions. How can this ever be done in an age of digital finance? Given the urgency, how can it be done in time? Given the sophistication of new technology, how can cross-border financial flows be managed? And anyway, how can any of these changes be brought about without international coordination? As the disappointing experience of UN climate conferences shows, the world's most powerful leaders appear unable to exercise international leadership. The president of the United States openly derides international collaboration to address major global challenges – including climate breakdown. So, given this political vacuum, who will drive global system change?

These are all justifiable questions and concerns. My answer is this: sooner rather than later the world is going to be faced by a shuddering shock to the system. I am not sure what that shock will be. It could be the flooding or partial destruction of a great city sited close to the rising seas. It could be widespread warfare, with an authoritarian and zealous climate denier leading the world into conflict. Or it could be (in my view, most likely) another collapse of the internationally integrated financial system. Given the rise in global temperatures and extreme weather events, the globalisation of authoritarian right-wing politics, and ever-increasing global economic imbalances, none of these scenarios fit the 'black swan' theory of difficult-to-predict events.[1] All three fall within the realm of normal expectations in history, science and economics.

So much for the shock itself. The question then will be: what comes next? How should society respond?

I attach particular importance to preparation for a fundamental disruption because of society's lack of readiness for the last shock: the Financial Crisis of 2007–09. The world's most powerful establishment figures, including central bankers, having been granted god-like status, neither predicted nor were prepared for that crisis. But, most dismayingly, leaders and activists that can loosely be defined as 'progressive' and on the left were equally unprepared – even when they were warned. Many, including the world's social democratic leaders, had aligned their political parties to the economics of neoliberalism – deregulation, privatisation and the restriction of workers' rights – and were often personally invested in the system. They were blindsided by events.

That lack of preparedness on the one hand, and collusion on the other, help to explain why the 2007–09 crisis did not provoke political responses that promised to build something different and better. The crisis stripped workers of livelihoods, decent wages, security and often a roof over their heads. But it did not threaten financialised capitalism. On the contrary: the crisis solidified the existing globalised financial order.

How therefore do we begin to think through an alternative to today's global financial system? The proposals outlined here draw on the experience of the 1930s, when capitalist economic structures were overhauled and the dominance of the finance sector was challenged. However, these proposals will not be comprehensive, and will leave many questions unanswered. That is in part because there can be no serious estimation of the conditions in which transformation will likely take place. Will planetary boundaries have been breached with catastrophic impacts? Will decision-makers have access to technology? Energy? Data? What form will social unrest take? Will institutions survive the hard shock? The future is unknown. This may be naïve of me, but I believe that a general strategy must nevertheless be developed, to encourage those with greatest expertise and experience to come forward and support work on improving and implementing the strategy. That is how we make a social revolution.

For progressives to be clear about the system change that is needed, we must be clear about what kind of a world we want. My assumption is that readers of this book share the view that our economic goal is for a 'steady state' economy (that is, an economy with a relatively stable, mildly fluctuating product of population and per capita consumption[2]) that helps to maintain and repair the delicate balance of nature, and respects the laws of ecology and physics (in particular thermodynamics). An economy that delivers social justice for all classes, and ensures a liveable planet for future generations. In consequence, this must be a world in which women's rights over their own bodies are paramount – for all the obvious reasons, but also so that human fertility can be managed. A world in which labour substitutes for carbon: a decarbonised economy will be a job-rich, labour-intensive economy. In it, we will do far more walking and cycling; we will not fly; we will give up meat and grow and consume local, seasonal, slow food. We will make and repair our own garments, rather than exploiting low-paid workers in far-off places. We will use both the sun's energy and human energy efficiently.

And, to do this, we will overturn the powerful ideology that drives the expansion of economic activity (see below) to unsustainable levels, the ideology of extreme individualism and competition, and will instead celebrate the uniquely human qualities of altruism, empathy and collective action. We will overturn what George Monbiot calls the 'spirit-crushing' and society-crushing capitalist system, destroying hope and common purpose. We will revive economic life at the community level by restoring the commons and by collectively managing the earth's scarce resources, including land – currently monopolised by the very few.[3]

First, a word about language. I have deliberately not referred here to a neoliberal term in wide use – 'growth' and its supposed opposite, 'degrowth'. Drawing on the work of George Lakoff and in particular his insights into the way framing influences reasoning, we now understand that *how* we say something is just as important, or perhaps more important, as *what* we say. One of his most valuable observations is that to negate a frame is to reinforce that frame. So, for example, 'degrowth' appears to be negating the neoliberal and relatively recent term 'growth.' In fact, by including it in our language, we are both repeating and reinforcing the concept. That is why the term is not used in this book, as I explain below.

The Global Economic Framework?

Given the goals outlined above, what would be the most appropriate global economic *framework* within which to maintain such an economy?

Should the Green New Deal be a single global plan? Implemented by a global authority? After all, as Herman Daly, pioneer of ecological economics and architect of 'steady state economics' has argued, the human economy is a subsystem sustained and contained by a delicately balanced *global* ecosphere, which in turn is fuelled by finite flows of solar energy.[4] The earth's life support systems do not recognise boundaries. In effect, we need to address the survival of the planet at a global level.

Or is the Green New Deal a set of principles that can only be applied to different regions and countries working collaboratively at the international level? A New Deal that relies on international cooperation, but that could take different conditions into account, and be implemented by local and nationally accountable institutions that reflect domestic conditions? And with the active participation of citizens?

I will argue for the latter framework. Namely, for the Green New Deal to be part of a collaborative rather than singular project. Transformation, in my view, must be implemented at levels of democratic accountability, and those levels fall within the political boundaries of nation states – or of nation states collaborating at regional level (e.g. European, African and Asian regional blocs.)

Financial globalisation has succeeded in its aims *because* regulatory democracy cannot function at the global level. Markets that operate in the financial stratosphere cannot be held to account by citizens, even when they effectively govern a nation's economy. In contrast, democracy can only function at the level of democratic institutions, and that means, invariably, at the level of the state. The reason is that public policy (for taxation, pensions, education, health, environmental regulation, etc.) requires boundaries. As Daly explains,

> Markets hate boundaries, but public policy, in the interest of the community, requires them . . . Since globalization is the erasure of national borders for economic purposes, it also comes close to being the elimination of national economic policy as well. In addition, it implies the eradication of international economic policy. Suppose all nations agreed to the Kyoto Accord. Then try to imagine how these nations could enforce domestically what they had agreed to internationally, when they have no control over their borders.
>
> International interdependence is to global integration as friendship is to marriage. All nations must be friends, but should not attempt multilateral marriage.[5]

Globalisation has created the meta-economic conditions that safeguard capitalism on the scale of the entire world. It is capitalism based on institutions designed not to liberate markets but to encase them, and by that means to promote exponential 'growth' in capital gains. William Brittain-Catlin paints a vivid picture of how the bankrupt company Enron made its capital gains:

> Enron had 692 subsidiaries incorporated in Cayman before it went bankrupt. It had about 200 other offshore companies in other tax havens around the world. Its offshore network was set up with the prime intention of avoiding tax in any country where it operated – the company even had a special unit working out the best offshore transactions for tax purposes. It was that kind of setup which made profits for Enron of nearly $2 billion between 1996 and 2000 – while the company only paid $17 million in tax.[6]

It was Enron's aggressive expansion 'offshore' that allowed it to become a secretive, deregulated, unaccountable global multinational. But there was more to what Enron was doing. The company engaged in complex trading on the world's capital markets. Derivatives were and are popular financial instruments for 'corporate financialisation' and Enron played around with derivatives. They are instruments that derive value from an underlying asset – just as an insurance policy derives its value from the insured asset (such as a property or car) and from the regular premiums paid on the insurance. Enron used derivatives and other financial instruments to do deals and swaps, switch into different currencies, and buy contracts. It was no longer a company that bought and sold energy. Instead it had become a bank – an offshore shadow entity that evaded laws and regulations wherever it operated, and gained an advantage.

But while globalisation benefits financialised corporates and the 1%, it also poses systemic risks to the rest of the world. That is because of the increased integration and interconnectedness of economies. Negative shocks in one part of the financial universe can spread, lightning-like, to corners of the globalised economy that bear no relation to or responsibility for the original shock. This system-wide connectedness is one of the reasons for the rise of popular insurgencies; they are angry reactions to threatening, apparently remote circumstances, beyond the control of citizens and their political representatives.

The big question is this: how to transform financialised capitalism? How to wrestle power over the great public good that is the monetary system away from the few that exercise private authority over the system? How to restore this great good to public, democratic authority?

First Step for System Change

This is where Donella Meadows's 'leverage points' will help guide our thinking. Leverage points are 'places within a complex system (a corporation, an economy, a living body, a city, an ecosystem) where a small shift in one thing can produce big changes in everything'.[7]

Systems don't exist in a vacuum. They arise from a paradigm – the mindset of a society, or, as Meadows explains: 'the shared idea in the minds of society, the great big unstated assumptions – unstated because unnecessary to state; everyone already knows them – constitute that society's paradigm, or deepest set of beliefs about how the world works.'[8]

Western societies have hardly questioned the system. Every so often, the costs of it – bankruptcies, the loss of secure jobs and decent wages – and the truth of who gains from the global financial architecture are laid bare. The 2007–09 Financial Crisis was one such event; the exposure of the Paradise Papers another.[9] But the results have been chastening. When the system has undermined or destroyed life chances, societies have often turned their anger and despair not against the banks, but against scapegoat targets such as immigrants and foreigners. They and their leaders have blamed countries like China. In the case of Britain, the blame fell on the European Union. As Karl Polanyi predicted, societies have yearned for 'strong men' – authoritarian leaders – to 'protect' them from apparently uncontrollable, globalised market forces.

So what are we to do? Paradigm shifts are hard to achieve. Resistance is, and will be, ferocious. Donella Meadows writes that 'societal responses to paradigm challenge have included crucifixions, burnings at the stake, concentration camps and nuclear arsenals.' Cheerful she is not. So, how to change paradigms?

> In a nutshell, you keep pointing at the anomalies and failures in the old paradigm, you keep speaking louder and with assurance from the new one, *you insert people with the new paradigm in places of public visibility and power*. You don't waste time with reactionaries: rather you work with active change agents and with the vast middle ground of people who are open-minded.[10]

Promote an Alternative Paradigm: Localisation

The Green movement, and within it, Green New Dealers, have for many years now promoted an alternative paradigm. It is framed as localisation, and echoes a paradigm that Keynes promoted way back in 1933 in a Yale journal, just a few months after the launch of Roosevelt's New Deal. In an essay titled 'National Self-Sufficiency', he set out the terms of a sustainable manifesto for a steady state economy. He began by sympathising with those who would minimize, rather than with those who would maximize, *economic entanglement* among nations. Ideas, knowledge, science, hospitality, travel – these are the things which should of their nature be *international*. But let *goods be homespun* whenever it is reasonably and conveniently possible, and, above all, *let finance be primarily national*.[11]

Economic entanglement among nations means both financial and trade entanglements. While trade will always be a characteristic human interaction, on the scale undertaken today, and under the terms prevailing, it is just not sustainable. Nor is it socially or ecologically just. As the British advocacy campaign, Global Justice Now, explains,

> current global trade, investment and financial regimes are based on powerful legal rules and norms that protect corporate interests. There are now 3,400 trade and investment binding treaties and agreements that protect transnational investments, including through secret courts which allow TNCs to sue governments without regard to their impact on people and planet. All these practices have led to violations of human rights and are continuing to prevent countries, especially in the global south, to realise their development aspirations and meet human rights obligations.

In the future, nations will continue to share and agree carbon targets, ideas, knowledge, skills, hospitality and regulatory standards and accords. But a key principle of the Green New Deal economy is surely that countries and their peoples be as self-sufficient as possible. That 'goods be homespun'.

This means that countries like Britain should cultivate their own green beans and sew their own clothes. They should not rely on poor countries draining water tables in order to grow green beans/red roses/tropical fruit for richer countries. This current system condemns workers in colonised and ex-colonised parts of the world to extremes of exploitation, only to satisfy the whims of fast-changing Western fashion.

The convenor of the British Green New Deal, Colin Hines, has for many years advocated a system of 'localisation' – the carefully managed refocusing of the global economy around local markets. Back in 2000 he published a book – *Localization: A Global Manifesto* – calling for the regeneration of local economies around the world. Localisation, he argued, would rehumanise trade, counteract globalisation's abuse of workers and the environment in both the North and the South, and foster self-reliance.[12]

Professor Tim Lang, professor of food policy at City University, has consistently argued that (re)localisation can meet the challenge of getting biodiversity from farm to plate, saving energy and cutting 'food miles'. The 'slow food' movement strives to preserve traditional and regional cuisine and encourages organic farming of plants and livestock characteristic of the local ecosystem. Modern consumers are already selective about the provenance of their food purchases.

At the heart of the slow food movement is the promotion of local produce and traditional gastronomy and food production methods. Conversely, this means the repudiation of fast food, industrial food production, and globalisation.[13] Agriculture practised on an industrial scale, geared towards exports to Western markets and using high levels of chemicals and synthetic fertilisers, is one of the main contributors to climate breakdown. Food production is estimated to cause between 19 and 29 per cent of global greenhouse gas emissions.[14] Dr Ian Fitzpatrick of Global Justice Now challenges the dominant orthodoxy on trade and development:

> We're led to believe that big agribusiness is the only way of feeding humanity. But evidence from small-scale, sustainable farming practices shows that they not only have greater yields, they also have multiple, positive knock-on effects like reducing greenhouse gas emissions, increasing employment and reducing the gender gap.[15]

What constitutes the boundary for localisation will depend on what goods or services are considered. Boundaries should reflect the views and needs of the communities concerned, but they will ultimately, in terms of allocation of the necessary supportive resources, be political decisions by those countries and the relevant regional blocs.

Powerful free-traders (at the WTO, World Bank and IMF) argue that free trade lowers prices and aids 'economic development'. As someone born in Africa, and still deeply attached to the continent, I beg to disagree. The continent itself is one of the richest in terms of natural resources. That is what makes it such a target for exploitation by richer countries. Africa is not poor, it is impoverished. In other words, it has been made poor, mainly by free trade, liberalisation and privatisation, all of which exacerbate the massive losses, extraction and slavery associated with colonial exploitation. As campaigners frequently assert, far from being backward and dependent on our help, Africa pays more money to rich countries than it receives in aid. We need to face up to the uncomfortable truth: Africa is aiding rich Western nations.[16]

To rebut the arguments of 'free traders', remember that trade is seldom free. Much of it is subsidised by governments via taxpayer-backed guarantees of bank lending and tax relief systems. The more powerful the nation, the more powerful are its government's 'export credit guarantees' that allow exporters to avoid 'free market' risk and instead depend on state backing.

So, 'let goods be homespun.' Let the localisation model be open to international exchange, mutual support and aid, while simultaneously minimising economic entanglement, and prioritising self-sufficiency where possible. That key paradigm shift is already happening. There are moves already towards a new system of greater self-sufficiency and localisation of economic activity. This can only be achieved if we commit ourselves to 'pointing at the anomalies and failures in the old paradigm, keep speaking louder and with assurance from the new one, and above all, let us *insert people with the new paradigm in places of public visibility and power*'.[17]

Let Money Be National

The financial globalisation project has been successful because its ideological backers have framed capital mobility as a 'freedom'. Such 'freedoms' can be traced back to neoliberal economists' belief that markets in money, trade and labour that have been transformed into global markets are thereby made more 'competitive'. Only global markets, they claimed, can be trusted to cut the costs of capital, trade, services and labour. But they went further and argued that capital mobility was a human right. According to Quinn Slobodian, Philip Cortney, an American neoliberal, 'linked capital control to the (human) right to leave a country'. He argued that the Universal Declaration of Human Rights should have gone further by including 'the right to free capital movement'. On a conservative estimate, a third of the world's wealth is held offshore, with 80 per cent of international banking transactions taking place there.[18] Brittain-Catlin and many others argue for capital to be brought back onshore, for one reason: to ensure that big corporations can be dragged out of 'the subterranean network of tax havens' and, as a consequence, be adequately taxed.[19]

How can this system change be achieved? A key leverage point in the complex and global financial system is to be found where capital crosses borders. Money (capital) pouring in and out of countries can be thought of as *flows* of capital. Money lodged in tax havens or other profit centres can be thought of as *stocks* of capital. To draw on systems thinking, we could imagine financial flows and stocks in terms of water flowing in and out of bathtubs. Anyone in a real bathtub naturally manages both the inflow and outflow. To fall asleep in the bath and allow the inflow to rise unchecked would be to risk drowning or flooding. Bathers don't just manage in and outflows, they use their senses to gauge the temperature of the water, and maintain a judicious balance between flows from hot and cold spigots.

In a positive feedback loop that guarantees 'success for the successful', capital mobility encourages 'sudden floods' and 'sudden stops' of capital. Capitalism abhors the use of 'faucets' or 'plugs' in managing cross-border capital flows. Rather than gauging and managing 'hot flows', speculators reinforce the direction of flows by piling in, herd-like, when financial 'temperatures' are rising. In this positive feedback loop, they raise the financial temperature further – until currency, asset and credit markets are disrupted, and the financial bathtub crashes through the economic equivalent of flooded floorboards, destroying the life-chances of millions of people below.

Capital mobility was, and is, a powerful weapon for capitalists. It allows actors in capital markets to move money quickly to where the highest capital gains can be made, regardless of the impact of those movements. It is designed to exploit and make massive gains from both small and large movements in the value of the bonds, currencies or interest rates of different nations, and create instability from gains and/or losses in these speculative activities. Financiers (in a process known as 'the carry trade') can borrow cheap in one nation and lend profitably at a much higher rate to another, invariably poorer nation, which in turn can lead to excessive credit expansion and soaring asset prices.

In addition, investors in capital markets can use the threat of capital flight to discourage democratic governments from adopting fiscal policies aimed at full, skilled and well-paid employment. (As this book goes to press, actors in capital markets are applying intense pressure on newly elected and radical president Lopez Obrador – Mexico's equivalent to Britain's Labour leader, Jeremy Corbyn.) Transnational corporations use the mobility of capital to engage in what is known as abusive transfer pricing – shifting profits from, say, a higher-tax to a lower-tax jurisdiction. The scale of profits from transfer pricing dwarfs the sums exposed in the Panama and Paradise Papers.

The powers enjoyed by the owners of mobile capital over democratic (and undemocratic) states, will make it challenging for governments and their people to regulate economic activity, limit 'growth' and create a steady state economy. It will be difficult to manage credit creation to finance energy and transport transformations, and to do so at low, sustainable rates of interest. It will be almost impossible to manage exchange rates so that knowledge and skills can be shared with the poorest countries. Lastly, it will be difficult to collect the tax revenues needed to help finance the transition to a sustainable economy.

In 2008 many countries that were neither instrumental in the crisis, nor at the centre of the financial collapse, watched as their currencies fell sharply and capital flooded like a tsunami out of emerging markets and into the country at the core of the crisis: the apparent 'safe haven' of the United States. As the crisis abated, and the Federal Reserve lowered interest rates to help American banks and corporations recover, the tsunami of capital reversed and transformed into the 'carry trade' as investors rushed into poorer, commodity-based economies with higher interest rates, in turn distorting *their* exchange rates, interest rates and economies.

Professor Jagdish N. Baghwati is an orthodox economist and a committed 'free trader'. In 1998 he wrote a famous and controversial paper: 'The Capital Myth: The Difference Between Trade in Widgets and Dollars'.[20] In it he argued that until the Asian crisis [of 1997] sensitised the public to the reality that capital movements could generate crises, many assumed that free capital mobility among all nations was exactly like free trade in their goods and services, a mutual-gain phenomenon. Hence restricted capital mobility, just like protectionism, was seen to be harmful to economic performance in each country, whether rich or poor.

Only globalised capital could reframe the term 'to protect one's economy' – protectionism – as harmful. Because, as Professor Baghwati explained, when a crisis hits, the downsides are enormous. To restore confidence, and lure capital back into the country, governments typically have to raise interest rates. This decimates home-bound firms that have borrowed in good faith, believing that interest rates would remain stable. To compensate for capital outflows, the government has to raise finance by selling off the nation's assets – the national airline, or ports, or the water system. These are flogged at knock-down prices in a 'fire sale' to foreign buyers with better access to funds. Finally, countries are forced by the IMF (or in the case of Europe, the European Commission) to open up their capital markets to Wall Street and the City of London, even though it was 'hot' money flows from these financial entrepots that 'played a principal role in their troubles in the first place'.

And, to compound these setbacks, countries permanently lose the political independence to run their economies as they deem fit, and in the interests of their citizens.

So capital mobility has many downsides. Among other flaws, as Professor Skidelsky has argued, 'Capital mobility has a tolerance for criminality.'[21] Drug dealers and criminals are particularly fond of capital mobility. Unregulated cross-border flows enable drug cartels to shift their illicit gains secretly across borders, untouched by customs authorities. On the most recent reckoning (2011), the global value of heroin trafficking according to the UN Office on Drugs and Crime was $68 billion. The global market for cocaine was worth $85 billion. Our experience of the rapid growth in drug dealing in the villages, towns and cities of Britain suggests that the UN's numbers may be a vast underestimation. They do not, of course, include the public health costs of this hugely profitable trade. They also do not include the associated costs when profits from drug trafficking are used to finance terrorism and insurgencies.

How to Manage Capital Mobility?

To manage capital flows, to slow them down or even block flows is more or less forbidden under a range of complex World Trade Organization rules and the myriad 'free trade agreements' (FTAs) and bilateral investment treaties (BITs) that many nations have signed up to over the past decade.[22] These agreements close down the ability of governments to exercise what is known in economics as 'policy autonomy' – the ability to decide on specific economic strategies. And these prohibitions are particularly strong for countries that have agreements with the United States. In other words, the imperialist power of the United States is used to enforce both the reality and the ideology of unfettered, globalised, capital mobility. During thirty years of increasingly frequent and grave financial crises, discussion and debate over how to manage the cross-border movement of capital was considered taboo. That is changing, slowly. Capital controls are actively discussed and indeed have been redesignated as 'capital flows management' by the IMF, even if the debate is limited to controls on inward flows. Debate on controls over outward flows – the capital flight that makes it so easy for corporations and corrupt elites to export both their legitimate and illicit gains – are still taboo. Nonetheless, remaining constraints can and will be loosened by another hard shock, for which we must be prepared, as leverage points can arise suddenly. Just as they did on the night of 9 November 1989, when the Berlin Wall fell and East Germans flooded across the border.

Now, without doubt, there are many powerful vested interests ready to argue that transformation of the current system is impossible. They will claim, and many of us will accept, that 'nothing can be done'. They will allege that owing to advances in modern technology, it is impossible to modify, never mind transform the globalized financial system.

But that is defeatism. The use or management of technology

is not the result of the churnings of some robotic algorithm; it is the result of economic, political and social decisions. If we choose to allow technology to dictate financial globalisation, that is a deliberate choice. We can just as easily choose to make technology work to tame financial globalisation. (And, as an aside: much of today's technology relies on the extraction of 'rare earths' and other scarce assets from some of the most impoverished countries in the world. These supplies are finite. The utopian dreams on which futuristic visions of technology are built are just that: utopian.)

Central Bankers as Gatekeepers

What is society's key leverage point for managing the powerful forces behind footloose capital flows? The straightforward answer is the central bank. Central bankers are gatekeepers for flows of capital in and out of countries, and for the entry of companies into a sovereign domain for the purpose of establishing a business. Admittedly the finance sector makes every effort to dodge the 'gatekeeper', and digital transfers make managing capital flows appear impossible. But the taxpayer-backed central bank working with the government has considerable powers.

First, in order to operate within a domain, financial institutions need to have permission, and to be registered with the central bank. For example, on the Bank of England's website, the Prudential Regulation Authority (PRA) lists all

1,500 banks, building societies, insurers and major investment firms registered with the Bank of England (BoE). That
registration and a careful approval process is necessary
before the firm can operate within the boundaries of the
United Kingdom. The Federal Reserve of the US also
requires banks and financial institutions to apply for member-
ship of the Federal Reserve System (Regulation H).[23]

That alone is a great power. Firms can be de-registered.
If their owners choose to flout capital controls, or any other
form of regulation, the central bank has the power to end
the firm's operations within the territory it regulates.

The government has additional powers. Its debt management office (sometimes based at the central bank, or alter-
natively in the finance ministry) issues government bonds
on behalf of the state's finance ministry. Government
bonds are in great demand, as, unlike private sector bonds,
sovereign bonds are among the world's safest assets and
are used by financiers as collateral – to leverage additional
borrowing. Bonds may vary in attractiveness, and therefore price, depending on economic conditions, but on the
whole they are very popular with investors and speculators
in global capital markets.

And there are levels of control in this trade that can be
regulated towards the Green New Deal. The treasury/
finance ministry decides which individuals or firms can
participate in the market to purchase or sell government
bonds. Those that wish to join 'the Approved Group' of
buyers need to satisfy certain criteria set down by the

government's debt management office. It is a power that can be deployed to exclude investors that prove unwilling to cooperate with government or to obey rules set by the public authorities – the central bank or finance ministry.

But there are other powers exercised by the taxpayer-backed central bank that are very important to global financiers and investors. One is access to a nation's currency. Another is access to central bank lending – or to the central bank's reserve-creation powers (central bank reserves are the equivalent of bank deposits) in exchange for assets. In 'shadow banking' or 'repo' markets that are relatively hidden from regulators, dealers in government bonds exchange government securities (collateral) on a short-term basis (usually overnight) in exchange for cash. This is known as a repurchase or 'repo' agreement. As Daniela Gabor has shown, largely unregulated repo markets have grown massively in volume, over a relatively short time, and are of systemic importance. They are private markets heavily dependent on government bond markets.[24] Around 75 per cent of repo transactions use government bonds as collateral.

Central bankers gain their powers from the strength of the domestic economy, and from the millions of taxpayers that effectively back their operations. The sovereign bonds of OECD countries are regarded as the safe collateral precisely because these sovereigns have never defaulted on their debts. But they have never defaulted largely because of the size and stability of their taxpayer base, and because millions of taxpayers (unlike global corporations) regularly pay their taxes.

These publicly backed resources, in great demand from financial institutions, are assumed to be automatically available to the private finance sector. That assumption must be challenged. Most governments are not powerless in the face of globalised capital markets. They possess public assets that the private finance sector cannot do without. These valuable resources should only be made available to the private finance sector on terms and conditions that benefit the taxpayers on whose regular payments the system depends.

Instead, powerful OECD governments and many emerging market economies have been hamstrung by an ideology that insists public interests should be subordinate to private interests, and mobile capital should remain unregulated – even though it has proved capable of causing grave, systemic harm to millions of innocent citizens.

Politicians, finance ministers and their central bankers have voluntarily given up important powers for managing and stabilising their own economies, preferring to abandon key levers of the economy to the whim of the 'invisible hand' – investors in capital markets.

If society is to achieve system change, that passive and defeatist mind-set has to change.

Capital controls take two forms: direct controls, or administrative controls, and indirect controls, or market-based controls.[25] Direct controls take the form of central bank prohibitions or quantitative controls over flows of money. Indirect controls discourage flows by applying taxes and making flows more costly.

If doubters argue that capital controls are impossible in today's high-tech world, they should be reminded that China deploys capital and exchange control measures all the time. The Chinese government does so in order to manage the exchange rate of its currency and thereby its economy.[26] Above all, it does so because it fears the social and political instability associated with economic shocks.

The controls used include restrictions on Chinese investment in foreign companies and overseas real estate. The central bank scrutinises cross-border payments to clamp down on over-invoicing. It also instructs banks to ensure that incoming and outgoing payments balance out, places strict limits on mainland Chinese purchases of Hong Kong insurance policies, and restricts so-called 'junket trips' to Macau, whose casinos have become a popular way of moving money out of mainland China. There was even a crackdown on individuals smuggling cash notes out of China. In May 2017, in a further attempt to close the loop on capital flight via its casinos, Macau imposed limits on cash withdrawals from ATMs by mainland Chinese residents.

To manage globalized capital mobility and ensure self-sufficiency, steady state economies must 'weaken the positive loops' that reward the winners of deregulated capital flows. That's what 'market-based controls', or taxes on flows, will do. They will simply slow down flows, putting sand in the wheels, while gathering revenues for the host government. Here again, civil society has long been on the case, with campaigns for a financial transactions tax, often called a 'Tobin' or Robin Hood tax.

Taxing capital flows does not mean that international transfers become impossible. It just means that large, 'hot' flows are managed. They are slowed, and, with central bank guidance, aimed at productive rather than speculative activity. The instruments are well known; many were widely used in the advanced economies during the 1960s and 70s. For a present-day example, as this goes to press, the New Zealand government has announced a ban on one particular cross-border financial flow: foreign money targeting the limited supply of existing New Zealand land and homes. Such investments are not for the purpose of occupying those homes, but for speculation that because of the finite nature of land in New Zealand, prices for land and property will rise forever. The second purpose is to prevent tax evasion by Chinese investors in particular. This flood of money helped inflate Auckland property prices to the highest in the world. It is hoped that the ban will cool property prices.

A key principle for steady state economies should be that capital flows are governed in order to, first, allow the authorities (the central bank and finance ministry) to tax those individuals and corporations that are economically active within the boundaries of a nation or region. Second, that governments should be free to manage a nation's exchange rate so that importers and exporters can depend on stable, predictable rates of exchange.

A third and crucial principle must be the management of interest rates by public authority (the central bank and finance ministry/treasury), so that rates on loans across the spectrum of lending in the domestic economy are fixed at levels affordable by home-based entrepreneurs and investors, instead of favouring the interests of remote, international investors and speculators.

Finally, it must be said that campaigns for 'tax justice' and 'fair taxation' – condemning 'illicit flows' away from impoverished countries – will only be effective if demands for proper taxes to be paid are backed up by the demand for offshore capital to be brought back onshore. And that can only be done by central bank intervention to manage cross-border capital flows.

Of course, such management of cross-border flows would best be achieved by international cooperation and coordination. But as the example of China shows, countries can also act unilaterally.

It will be impossible for governments to finance the transition to a steady state economy in a world of capital mobility. Management of international capital flows are therefore fundamental, not just to the financing of the transition to a steady state economy, but also to the survival of the planet.

4

The Green New Deal Economy

The Green New Deal is not a brand in the commercial sense of the word, demanding 'brand loyalty'. Nor is it a binding manifesto that commands absolute adherence. However, while the British and American GNDs differ in some respects, both are built on key principles. The following economic principles can fairly be said to underpin the British Green New Deal and are almost entirely shared with its American counterpart.

Principle Number One: A Steady State Economy

An economy that sustains life on earth will be a steady state economy and will not exceed the nine ecological boundaries: stratospheric ozone depletion; loss of biosphere integrity (biodiversity loss and extinctions); chemical pollution and the release of novel entities; climate change; ocean acidification; freshwater consumption and the global hydrological cycle; land system change; nitrogen and phosphorus flows to the biosphere and oceans; atmospheric aerosol loading.[1]

Minimising waste by adopting closed loop recycling methods will be central to a steady state economy, as will the rapid development of mutually supporting, circular energy and resource networks where people live and work. Reuse, remanufacture, and secondary material supplies can address resource insecurity. Some products are already designed to be converted back to raw material, allowing for repeated use and the remaking of the same product over and over again. Such activity will ensure that the stock of physical capital is kept steady, while economic and social activity builds and rebuilds overall system health.

Herman Daly, the world's leading proponent of the steady state economy, argues that it is composed of two physical populations – people and artefacts – existing as elements of a larger, natural system. Artefacts (physical capital) yield services that serve human needs (as opposed to 'wants'), and so do people.

> These two populations may be thought of as a fund, like a lake, with an outflow necessitated by death and depreciation, which can be reduced but never eliminated. The outflow is offset by an inflow of births and production which may exceed, fall short of, or equal the outflow.[2]

In a steady state, or circular, economy what is held constant is the capital stock in the broadest physical sense of the term, including capital goods, the total inventory of consumer goods, and the population of human bodies. What will not be held constant is culture, care, love, inheritance, knowledge, goodness, ethical codes, empathy, intelligence, judgement and so forth – embodied in human beings.[3]

> Not only is quality free to evolve, but its development is positively encouraged . . . If we use 'growth' to mean quantitative change, and 'development' to refer to qualitative change, then we may say that a steady-state economy develops but does not grow, just as the planet earth, of which the human economy is a subsystem, develops but does not grow.[4]

Principle Number Two: Limited Needs, Not Limitless Wants

The Green New Deal's overwhelming approach to earth systems breakdown is to reverse the dominant paradigm, and place strict limits on the apparently limitless consumption of capitalist economies and societies. At the same time the GND will address and meet society's more limited *needs*. All individuals, everywhere in the world, at all times present and future, have certain basic needs. These must be met in order for people to avoid harm, to participate in society and to reflect critically upon the conditions

– including their natural surroundings – in which they find themselves. Basic needs are then the universal preconditions for effective participation in any form of social life.[5]

Drawing on the work of the economist Ian Gough, human needs, unlike consumer preferences, 'wants' and happiness, are not morally neutral. They imply ethical obligations on individuals and on claims of justice – universal rights and obligations – from social institutions. In the Anthropocene, they assert standards of *sufficiency* and the moral priority of human needs (present and future) over consumer wants or preferences.[6]

The Green New Deal, therefore, aims to satisfy human needs, not wants. While survival is the most basic human need, all people require health and autonomy for effective social participation. Hence Alexandria Ocasio-Cortez's demand for 'Medicare for All' is fundamental to the US Green New Deal, and why, in the UK, the call for the preservation of a well-funded NHS is fundamental.

In addition to health, the GND defines the following basic needs as essential: adequate, nutritious food and water; protective housing; non-hazardous physical and work environments; security in childhood; significant primary relationships; physical security; economic security; safe birth control and child-bearing; basic education. To optimise these needs, argues Professor Gough, societies require freedom from oppression (civic and political rights); freedom to satisfy needs; and freedom of political expression.[7]

Principle Number Three: Self-Sufficiency.

As previously highlighted, within an international frame-work of cooperation and coordination, and with support and wealth transfers to poor countries suffering the consequences of centuries of colonisation and the industrialisation of rich countries, a steady state economy will encourage societies to establish self-sufficiency. Countries, especially those in the Global South, will be free to throw off colonial chains, and become more autonomous in terms of economic policy-making. All nations will aim at self-sufficiency in the provi-sion of human needs, goods and services for their citizens. While ideas, knowledge, inventions and art will be interna-tional, 'goods will be homespun'.

At an individual level, private sufficiency will be comple-mented by public luxury. As George Monbiot argues, the expansion of public wealth creates more space for every-one; the expansion of private wealth reduces it, eventually damaging most people's quality of life.

> In co-housing developments, people own or rent their own homes but share the rest of the land. Rather than chopping the available space into coffin-sized gardens in which a child cannot perform a cartwheel without hitting the fence, the children have room to run around together while the adults have space to garden and talk. Communal laundries release living space in people's homes. Carpools reduce the need for parking. Isolation gives way to conviviality.[8]

Principle Number Four: A Mixed-Market Economy

Extraordinary levels of collective effort will be required if societies are to achieve the transformation of their economies away from dependence on fossil fuels and the extraction of the earth's finite assets. The scale of such efforts will be comparable to that of a nation urgently embarking on the collective effort of defence in the face of impending war.

A discussion of the role of the state in implementing the Green New Deal is for another book. Suffice to say that, as in wartime, the state is the most appropriate institution for financing, mobilising and implementing the huge effort of economic transformation. A state with regulatory and taxation powers over different sectors will be in a position to use these powers to end dependence on fossil fuels, and to ensure planetary boundaries are not breached. Regulation will be essential if we are to eliminate market incentives to disrupt ecosystem services.

Ideally the transformation project should be participative, decentralising and anti-bureaucratic. In their book, *The People's Republic of Walmart*, Leigh Phillips and Michal Rozworski point out that big corporations ignore all the ballyhoo about free market competition in running their companies.[9] Centralised planning and above all trust, openness and cooperation along the supply chain – rather than competition – are fundamental to the success of one corporation, Walmart, that is simultaneously the most exploitative of labour and the ecosystem. Planning, trust, transparency, participation and cooperation in pursuit of quite different goals will be fundamental to the Green New Deal.

We recognise, however, that transformation of the economy requires more than the collective efforts of the state. Market transactions will complement, support and gain from the activities of the state. Human societies have at least 5,000 years' experience of transacting through markets and regulating those markets. The Green New Deal is best delivered by a mixed economy – in which the state undertakes those activities most appropriate for collective action, while the market will facilitate the transaction of goods and services provided within the steady state framework.

The way this could work will be for the state to invest in the big transformational projects – for example, the acquisition and reforestation of large swathes of land, the building of mass transit, and the retrofitting of buildings. Such public investment will benefit local contractors and entrepreneurs who know the area, can recruit and train a locally based workforce to undertake the decarbonising work, and thereby generate income for the firm itself, but also for its employees and the local community.

Principle Number Five: A Labour-Intensive Economy

As implied above, the Green New Deal economy will be labour-intensive. Activities currently driven by energy derived from fossil fuels will run on renewable energy. Those activities that cannot be powered by the sun's energy will be undertaken by human energy: labour. Hence the US Green New Deal's promise of a 'job guarantee' for everyone, and the British GND promise to mobilise a 'carbon army' of workers to undertake and maintain the transformation. Both public and private sectors will create highly skilled jobs for, for example, physicists, climatologists, dendrologists, arboriculturists, civil engineers, chemical engineers, electricians, welders, bus drivers, computer software engineers, millwrights and sheet metal workers, as well as hairdressers, tailors, designers, coffee merchants and retailers, cleaners and carers – to name but a few.

During the Second World War, millions of women were drawn into the labour force. Likewise, millions of unemployed and under-employed people will be drawn into the vast areas of work needed for the transformation of the economy to a steady state. There will be no room for discrimination on grounds of gender, race or ability. The promise of the GND is that the workforce will be rewarded with meaningful tasks; resourced with skills, training and higher education. And, crucially, workers will earn decent wages and incomes.

Therefore, the economy will be geared towards addressing their finite human needs. Decent wages backed up by the provision of universal basic services, like health, education, housing and care will not only create meaningful work, they will also be necessary to keep the economic system in balance. The aim will be to abolish the obscene inequalities characteristic of late-stage capitalism.

UBI vs UBS

Because of the insecurity and volatility caused by financial-ised globalisation; because of rising inequality, falling real pay and precarious work, the campaign for a Universal Basic Income (UBI) appears to offer a positive solution. UBI is a genuine attempt to build political power to tackle injustice and inequality, by ensuring the state distributes a basic income – to everyone.

My unease with UBI stems from concerns about this distribution. UBI is provided regardless of need, as Anna Coote and colleagues at the New Economics Foundation explain.[10] While the universal sum agreed upon (and the huge financial burden this will place on the state) may not be enough to help those in severe need, UBI will be a generous gift to the affluent who don't need it. It is the expenditure equivalent of a flat tax and as such is regressive. But the consequences of funding a UBI are hefty – well in excess of the entire welfare budget of most countries. As the general secretary of the trade union Public Services International, Rosa Pavanelli, argues, even if we were able to build the political movement required to raise that extra finance – would we choose to hand so much of it to the wealthiest? There is no evidence that UBI will help to increase the bargaining power of workers and trade unions, or solve the problems of low pay and precarious work. On the contrary, some would point out that what was meant to be a floor could become a ceiling. This was Marx's objection to the Speenhamland system: a society with a basic income has no pressure to pay employees a good wage, because the bottom constraint, subsistence, has fallen away. And, as Nathan Heller notes, we see such an effect in the gig economy, where companies pay low wages while celebrating that the work is flexible and assuming that workers have income from elsewhere. [11]

Public services, in contrast, are a strong vehicle for redistribution. According to Oxfam, they provide the poorest people with the equivalent of 76 per cent of their post-tax income.[12] They are a more effective and efficient redistributive tool than cash transfers. But most important perhaps for the GND is that services embody the means to build cooperation and solidarity – which will be much needed in a world in which earth systems are failing. They bring people together and by so doing manifest the collective ideal: people pooling resources, caring and helping each other to cope with risks they could never manage alone.

Principle Number Six: Monetary and Fiscal Coordination for a Steady State Economy

Next, we must reverse neoliberalism's elevation of monetary policy over fiscal policy.

This is a mistake often repeated inadvertently by 'monetary reformers'. Under the GND, the state's monetary and fiscal institutions and policies will work in tandem to support society as a whole, not just the finance sector. Our understanding of the macroeconomy (the economy in aggregate) over the microeconomy (such as the economy of the household) owes everything to Keynes. Before Keynes, economists thought of the economy largely in 'micro' terms – and many still do. Keynes was concerned with the macroeconomy because he was overwhelmingly concerned to create conditions that would increase employment. Full employment is fundamental to the Green New Deal.

To create full employment, the monetary authorities will, via the central bank, provide ('macro') clients like the government, banks and pension funds with loans and deposits, just as commercial banks provide loans and deposits to ('micro') firms and individuals. This is not to suggest that central banks will finance government spending; however, their exchange of government bonds for central bank reserves will help keep the cost of government borrowing low. (I expand on this point below.)

In a 1934 essay, Keynes asked, 'Can America Spend Its

Way into Recovery?'[13] His answer was that when the government borrows in order to spend, it undoubtedly gets the nation into debt, but the debt of a nation to its own citizens is a very different thing from the debt of a private individual. It's a macroeconomic issue, not a microeconomic one. The nation is the aggregate of citizens who comprise it – no more and no less – and to owe money to them is not very different from owing money to oneself, wrote Keynes, concluding that 'insofar as taxes are necessary to shift the interest payments out of one pocket and into the other, this is certainly a disadvantage; but it is a small matter compared with the importance of restoring normal conditions of prosperity'.

The GND economy will not be debt-free, but its credit creation systems will be balanced by tax revenues gained from employment, used to repay loans to prevent the build-up of debt and deficits. Thus a 'steady state' financial system is one that creates a virtuous circle, one we will explore below.

The monetary authorities will also ensure the value of the currency remains stable, will regulate the private banking system, and manage the rate of interest over society's spectrum of borrowing. This will include short- and long-term loans, differentiating between safe and risky loans, and the price (interest) on loans in relation to inflation.

The public authorities (in the form of the finance ministry) in charge of fiscal policy will use loan-finance to spend and support investment on productive activity that will transform the economy away from fossil fuels, create jobs and generate tax revenues. Public investment will provide the goods and services needed by society and the ecosystem, and by stimulating both private and public sector employment will also generate the income needed to fund this transformation. Finally, employment will generate tax revenues – to be used to repay the government's borrowing. Just as now, tax revenues will not finance that initial investment or activity. Instead they will arise as *a consequence* of government (and private) expenditure, and will be used to repay public debt. It would be a fine thing if politicians understood that the best way to raise taxes is not by hiking them, but by expanding skilled, well-paid employment. As we all know from our own experience, once employed, workers are taxed. The higher our income the more we are (or should be) taxed. Part of the income from employment returns to government to pay for the loan-financed public expenditure that helped create the skilled, well-paid jobs, and that was spent on education, health, transport, reforestation, and so on.

Nonetheless, there is one form of taxation that we should be cautious about. Carbon taxes generate revenue and may be necessary to alter behaviour, but like flat taxes, they are largely regressive. They could have an important but limited role to play as part of a far more fundamental reshaping of the economy, but to be effective they should be targeted at the biggest emitters. We know that the richest 10 per cent are responsible for half of the total lifestyle

consumption carbon emissions in the world, while the
poorest half contribute a mere ten per cent. Slashing the
carbon emissions of wealthy people to the European average (not the Malawian average!) would go a long way to
resolving the world's carbon emissions crisis, as Professor
Kevin Anderson has argued. If 90 per cent of the population did nothing, then carbon emissions would be cut by 30
per cent.[14] We have only to recall the 'morally bereft' CEOs
that visited Davos in January 2019 in dozens of private jets
to grasp that it is the 10 per cent that should be targeted not
the rest. Neoliberal economists resort to carbon taxes and
carbon trading as the first and only way to change behaviour and discourage carbon use. Such taxes shift the burden
of carbon adjustment on to the poor and relatively powerless. At the same time the politically powerful discourage
large-scale public investment in alternative systems. The
flaws and corrupt practices exposed by the European
market-based 'cap and trade' schemes, and the insurgency
of the French *gilets jaunes*, have shown that this approach
worsens conditions, and almost surely delays transformation away from a fossil fuel-based economy.

Instead, in the spirit of the Marshall Plan, massive investment in infrastructure to tackle earth systems breakdown
must be *frontloaded*. In other words, urgent transformation
will be more easily achieved if governments working with
the private sector rapidly construct alternatives to the
current financial, transport, energy, built environment, and
agricultural systems. Once alternative systems are in place

for use by citizens, only then will it be necessary to use carbon taxes to incentivise or discourage different behaviours by the public.

Principle Number Seven: Abandon Delusions of Infinite Expansion

In order to maintain a steady state, and to prevent inflation, it will be important to *pace* economic activity: not only to avoid exceeding the limits of the ecosystem, but also to avoid the inflation of prices. Inflation arises when levels of economic activity – investment, employment, output – exceed the capacity of the economy. While employment of labour will be expanded under the Green New Deal, the rate at which jobs are created during the transition to a steady state economy will be important. Economic activity must be kept steady, to not exceed the capacity of the economy. If it were to do so, it would cause inflation which would in turn erode the value of income.

Financialised capitalism assumes the global economy has infinite capacity for the addition and consumption of goods and services; hence the obsession with 'growth'. The key advocate for the concept of 'growth' was Samuel Brittan, lead commentary writer of the *Financial Times*. In the 1960s he proudly identified himself as a 'growthman'. At a time of full employment, he and economists at the rich nations club – the OECD – raised the bar of economic expectations. Full employment was not a sufficient goal, they reasoned, and was to be abandoned. Instead, the concept of growth as the objective of all economic policy was adopted by the newly founded OECD in 1961. An extraordinary 50 per cent growth target was set for Britain for the whole of the 1960s. As Geoff Tily remarks,

> The world had officially been set a systematic and improbable target: to chase growth. Nobody seems to have paused to consider whether growth derived as the rate of change of a continuous function was a meaningful or valid way to interpret changes in the size of economies over time.[15]

'Growth' was revived and reinvented by economists like Sam Brittan in the 1960s to force the real economy to expand at the same unsustainable rate as the speculative financial economy was 'growing' at that time. Capital gains from speculation and rent-seeking can rise spectacularly, whereas profits from investment in real economic activity can both rise and fall. To force the real British economy to expand at the same rate as capital gains made from deregulated financial speculation meant the OECD had to force unrealistic 'growth rates' on an economy already at full capacity (enjoying full employment). It was that unwise, neoliberal advice that led to the inflationary era of the 1970s – for which both Keynes and Labour governments have been blamed! Keynes would have turned in his grave at policies for credit and interest rate deregulation and excessive expansion at a time of full employment. It should come as no surprise that this led to the rise of inflation – which was then blamed on the workforce who sought to match wage rises to price rises. Orthodox economists were not held responsible at the time, and still avoid accountability today for deliberately inflating the economy in the 1970s.

GDP, 'Growth' and the Ecosystem

The subject of economic expansion has been much studied and written about by philosophers, theologians, scientists and environmentalists as well as economists. John Stuart Mill first launched the idea of a 'stationary state' in 1857 – a system of zero growth in population and physical stock, but with advances in technology and ethics.[16] Later, Nicholas Georgescu-Roegen, student and protégé of Joseph Schumpeter, explained the relevance of thermodynamics to economics: the physical fact that mankind can neither create nor destroy matter or energy, only transform it.[17] When we burn a log fire, the logs, heat, ash, smoke, and invisible gases generated do not disappear. They are merely transformed from a usable form of energy to an unusable form, which cannot be recovered. Entropy is the measure of that unusable energy.

For Georgescu-Roegen, the terms 'production' and 'consumption' obscure the fact that nothing is created and nothing is destroyed in the economic process: everything is simply transformed. And because our ecosystem is both finite and closed, the growth of the economy – a sub-system of the ecosystem – is limited by this finitude. Georgescu's work was seminal to the establishment of ecological economics as an academic sub-discipline in economics.

In his book *The Growth Delusion*, David Pilling, a distinguished *Financial Times* journalist, recently brought added urgency to this long-standing debate about the 'cult of growth'. One catalyst for the book was Pilling's experience as head of the FT's Tokyo bureau from 2002 to 2008. Japan, he observes, is

> regularly written about as though it were some kind of basket case stuck in perpetual stagnation and without the wits to haul itself out of misery . . . Japan's supposed misery – as measured by nominal GDP – really didn't feel like misery at all. Unemployment was extremely low, prices stable or falling, and most people's living standard rising. Communities were intact, certainly in comparison to those in America, Britain and France. Crime was low, drug use almost non-existent, the quality of food and consumer goods world class, and health and life expectancy among the highest in the world. And yet, viewed through the prism of economics, Japan was an abject failure.[18]

Japan's lack of economic 'growth' turned out to be a flawed measure of its actual condition.

However, while Pilling takes sharp aim at 'the cult of

growth', it quickly becomes clear that the real target of his book is a single, totemic number: the aggregate measure of the value of a nation's goods and services produced during a given period – Gross Domestic Product, or GDP. A number, he argues, that is the driving force behind the cult of endless, exponential growth. Growth as measured by GDP, he and others claim, has become the overlord of measures. It is the number used to define success and has been elevated to an article of faith for most politicians.

And yet: does blame for the 'cult of growth' really lie with *a measure*? It is self-evidently false that GDP offers any measure of national wellbeing, for, as Bobby Kennedy once declared, 'it measures neither our wit nor our courage, neither our wisdom nor our learning, neither our compassion nor our devotion to our country . . . It measures everything, in short, except that which makes life worthwhile.'[19]

But surely it is not just the failure of measurement that is the problem with 'growth'? We will always have to measure the economy, especially if we want to manage it and prevent economic activity from expanding relative to the capacity of the ecosystem. Instead the problems we face are the political decisions that determine what should be counted as GDP, and importantly the ideology of endless expansion. It is those drivers that really matter, not the measurement. The fact is GDP is an inadequate measure of the economy and of all that society values. It can be likened to the speed dial on a car dashboard. But to criticise the dial – and not the speed at which the car is travelling, or the driver applying the pedal – is to miss the point of 'growth'. There can be no doubt that today's globalised and financialised economy has sped us all towards a range of dangerous roadblocks – the earth's planetary boundaries. Tackling these threats requires fundamental economic policy changes, not just adjustments to our system of economic measurement.

Before the Second World War, the concept of 'growth' scarcely existed.[20] Instead economists discussed and debated *levels* of economic activity. Was the level of employment, investment, or output too high, or too low? If so, what change was required in economic policy?

Perhaps the most serious criticism of 'growth' is that made by Herman Daly: that it ignores finitude, entropy and ecological interdependence, because the concept of throughput (the maximum rate at which something can be processed) is absent. Rather, 'growth' is conceived as an 'isolated circular flow of exchange value'.

> It is as if one were to study physiology solely in terms of the circulatory system without ever mentioning the digestive tract. The dependence of the organism on its environment would not be evident. The absence of the concept of throughput in the economists' vision means that the economy carries on no exchange with its environment.[21]

So let us all banish the term 'growth'. But just as importantly, let us also avoid the term 'degrowth', because by negating 'growth', we simply reinforce the concept of growth.[22] Better to argue for the positive alternative: a steady state economy.

The Steady State Economy

The size of the steady state economy will equal the size of the human presence in the ecosystem, as measured by population times per capita resource use. Herman Daly clearly explains the dilemmas we will face when determining the size of the steady state economy, by means of a perfect analogy:

> The micro allocation problem is analogous to allocating optimally a given amount of weight in a boat. But . . . there is still the question of the absolute amount of weight the boat can carry. This absolute optimal scale of load is recognized in the maritime institution of the Plimsoll line. When the watermark hits the Plimsoll line the boat is full, it has reached its safe carrying capacity . . . as the absolute load is increased, the water line will reach the Plimsoll line even for a boat whose load is optimally allocated. Optimally loaded boats will still sink under too much weight – even though they may sink optimally![23]

What is the work that must be done if we are to bring to an end our fast-fashion, 'take-make-waste' linear economy, and still remain above the earth's equivalent of the Plimsoll line?[24] How many will have to be employed to design out waste and pollution, keep some products and materials in use, and regenerate natural systems? At what cost must the world's temples to consumption – *Vogue*, Waitrose, Amazon, Walmart, to name but a few – be closed down? If we can reinvent everything, as Ellen MacArthur suggests, how many people must we set to work to do so?[25]

For these calculations we will need the help of statisticians, economists, experts in the fields of technology, engineering, energy, transport, agronomy, education, health, and many more. Much of the present economy may have to be dismantled, shut down, sealed up. Assessments and inventories of the work will have to be made. Labour – both physical and intellectual – will have to be counted, trained and allocated to these big tasks.

The great question for environmental macroeconomics is one of optimal scale. What is the potential scale of an economy that can be operationalised within safe ecological limits? How big should the subsystem of the economy be, relative to the total ecosystem? Countries will differ, and this author is in no position to judge the size of individual economies, except to argue that we should keep the human share sufficiently low so as not to disrupt the life-support systems essential to survival.

Nor can the 'invisible hand' be trusted, because while it may be good at managing supply and demand for some goods and services, it has no power to set limits to the scale of the economy, relative to the ecosystem. We need an economic Plimsoll line that caps the macroeconomy at a sustainable level. UN scientists have already indicated where that line should be drawn in terms of temperature rises, and experts at the Stockholm Environment Institute have calculated the cuts in emissions that rich countries have to make and the room that is available for low-income countries to continue emitting.[26]

And while it is clear that the richest countries have to make the deepest emission cuts and provide the most finance if we are to fairly share the responsibility of limiting climate breakdown, it is not clear to this author that calculations as to the optimal size of individual economies have been made. In other words, what levels of investment, employment and output are permitted above the 'Plimsoll line' that would keep a given economy steady?

In order to know whether the Green New Deal is affordable; in order to know what is needed to finance the GND, it will be necessary, first, for experts to make an assessment of the potential and optimal scale of the economy. That Plimsoll line will have to be drawn across individual economies as well as the global economy, with much cooperation in achieving balance and justice across the world. Once that line is determined, the tasks of transformation can be defined, and the scale of global financing required made evident.

5

A Steady State Economy

We must acknowledge that we do not have all the solutions now.
We must admit that we do not have the situation under control.
And we must admit that we are losing this battle. We must stop
playing with words and numbers because we no longer have time
for that.

Greta Thunberg, Vienna Climate Conference,
1 June 2019

A *credible* economic plan is necessary to finance the vast transformation necessary to save the planet, and do so urgently. For the plan to be adopted widely, it has to ring true with the wider public, whose intelligence must never be underestimated. The plan must be honest and sound enough to cut through the fierce resistance and, at times, defeatism that will come from all quarters.

My approach in this chapter draws on the experience of working with the international Jubilee 2000 campaign for the cancellation of more than $100 billion of debt owed by more than thirty of the world's poorest countries. We began as a small, under-financed organisation with just a few supporters and only four years in which to achieve our goal. We faced stubborn resistance. The fiercest opposition came from international creditors, including private investors, such as New York–based 'vulture funds', but also public, governmental creditors. These included the world's richest and most powerful governments that had guaranteed loans to low-income countries. Their opposition to our underresourced campaign was buttressed and given intellectual heft by the media. But also by many smart, experienced but highly orthodox economists at the Washington-based International Monetary Fund and World Bank, as well as those at the French treasury, home to the Paris Club of sovereign creditors.

It was a daunting assignment. We had to get both our economic and financial analysis right. We had to contend with, and overcome, sophisticated and well-informed intellectual as well as ideological opposition. But we did it, and against all the odds. Our success came, to my mind, because our case 'rang true'. Not just with the 24 million people that signed our petition to leaders of the world, but also, eventually, with government finance ministries and even those smart economists at the IMF. Even the

Financial Times changed its tune in the end and backed our campaign. Our case rang true because our analysis was rigorous, our facts and evidence accurate, and our arguments sound.

If the Green New Deal is to succeed, we must win the public's confidence anew. Fundamental to winning that confidence will be realistic, rational and brutally honest answers to the public's questions, and scepticism about any plans for 'unorthodox monetary tricks'.

One question we will face is this: can the system really be transformed in such a short time?

The honest answer is probably 'no'. It may already be too late.

Another still honest answer is a provisional 'yes': it may be very late, but societies have transformed abruptly before; for example, under the New Deal as discussed earlier; second in the rushed preparation by Britain to fight the Second World War, or third, when President Nixon swiftly and unilaterally dismantled the post-war international financial architecture (Bretton Woods) in 1971. Led by political leaders, scientists and activists that have a real grasp of the scale of the emergency humanity faces, and with a proper sense of the danger and the need for urgency, we could still make drastic changes. We may still have time.

Another question will be: how can we pay for this rapid transition away from dependence on fossil fuels, when politicians constantly warn 'there is no money'?

We can answer that question with supreme confidence: in societies with sound monetary systems, there can never be a shortage of finance. And for those that do not have sound monetary systems, the world has vast quantities of savings that can be deployed to help finance the transition in impoverished countries.

Then: can our monetary and other public *institutions* survive earth systems breakdown?

Probably not. But if we understand the importance of these institutions as a collective and *public good*, just as important as, say, the public good that is our sanitation system, then our monetary institutions will have a better chance of surviving to help finance the transformation.

How can we pay for it without stoking inflation, worsening the ecological emergency and hurting those we know are least responsible for the situation? In other words, how can we both lower emissions but also ensure equity for the low emitters? The low emitters include both those who live among us and the millions who live a long way from where we live, who are largely non-white and non-Western – all of whom are among the least responsible for the climate crisis.

These are more difficult questions to answer. But it is worth reminding ourselves that, given the scale of global warming and the latest evidence on mass extinctions, so much about the future is uncertain. It is not possible to create a detailed blueprint for the financing of a global, regional or national GND that might need to change over time. Nonetheless, following Greta Thunberg's advice, we will cease playing with numbers based on existing, flawed GDP measurements and uncertainty about the future. For too long, economists like William Nordhaus have used numbers as part of cost–benefit analyses to discount and dollarize damage caused by climate change versus the cost of preventing climate change. When the numbers showed the cost of prevention was greater than the estimated cost of climate change, they effectively argued for the 'cheaper' version: planetary breakdown![1]

Instead we will outline the key concepts and key stages in planning a steady state economy. We will draw on sound monetary theory and on past experience, but also on the more recent scientific understanding of the state of the ecosystem in which an economic strategy must be developed and implemented.

GND Blueprint

There have been various attempts at blueprints for financing the Green New Deal. The first analysis was rushed out by the conservative American Action Forum (AAF) just two weeks after the congressional launch of the GND. The AAF is led by Douglas Holtz-Eakin, until recently head of the US Congressional Budget Office.[2] A second study, based on Keynes's famous essay *How to Pay for the War*, was published in May 2019 by economists Yeva Nersisyan and L. Randall Wray at the US-based Levy Institute: *How to Pay for the Green New Deal*.[3] While the Levy Institute's paper is a serious investigation and a careful attempt to cost the US GND, the AAF paper adopts strawman arguments to spread alarm. It is unbalanced and predictably orthodox, tentatively and superficially examining likely expenditure without acknowledging how the visionary programme might generate income, too. While the public may initially be taken in by such scaremongering, we are confident they can discern when a political, rather than a rigorously economic, point is being made.

The uncertainties that bedevil the attempt to develop an economic strategy were highlighted by the Holtz-Eakin paper. It noted that the US Green New Deal, like the British GND, prioritises the retrofitting of every building in the US. The purpose would be to cut back emissions, and improve energy efficiency. At the same time, like the British GND, the call is for the electricity grid to be sourced from 100 per cent renewable energy – wind, solar, hydro, geothermal electricity, as well as the development of improved battery storage and energy efficiency. The ultimate conversion to alternative energy would make the former activity of retrofitting redundant.

Therefore, to understand how to pay for the GND, and prepare a budget, it is necessary to understand the hierarchy of priorities for specific sectors. First, what exactly is our (national, regional or city's) carbon budget? Should we begin by raising carbon taxes on the 20 per cent of global citizens that account for 70 per cent of emissions, as

Kevin Anderson argues? Given the emergency, will the US Green New Deal government target its citizens (who average 16.4 tonnes of CO_2 per person) by imposing a tax of $1,000 per tonne of CO_2?[4] That would quickly generate revenues (which would just as quickly decline as emissions decline) – and this relatively small group of high emitters would bring the world closer to zero quicker than any other measure. Will the GND start by transforming the electricity grid, or by retrofitting houses? Would the sensible approach be to do both? Or should we begin actively to decarbonise, by the reforestation of vast areas of farmland? Will these priorities be blown away by the need to address sea-level rises, the flooding of coastal communities and cities and the likely social and political unrest associated with natural disasters?

These uncertainties make it highly improbable that we can provide simple and unchanging, accurate calculations. But we can address key economic concepts to underpin the development of a 'steady state' economic strategy.

Developing a Strategy for a Steady State Economy

Given the considerable uncertainties, if a reader were in the near future to be appointed finance minister, treasury secretary or even prime minister of a country, what economic strategy should they adopt to implement the Green New Deal?

The strategy assumes that this finance minister, supported by a governor of the central bank, has challenged the globalisation model, and adopted monetary tools and regulations for managing cross-border capital flows. Having slain the dragon that is globalised finance, she therefore has a fair degree of policy autonomy over key economic levers; in particular, the management of cross-border flows; the exchange rate of her nation's currency and the rate of interest for loans across the spectrum of borrowing for both the public and private sectors.

In order to decide on how much, and what economic activity is viable, the finance minister will need to consider two kinds of capacity: the potential capacity of the economy, and the available capacity of the ecosystem. In other words, in order to develop an economic strategy she will need not one, but two budgets: a carbon budget and a budget for expenditure and income.

This challenge drives us right back to the earlier chapter on the global system. To understand the 'Plimsoll line' of a region or nation, we need an international agreement on the permitted global level of carbon dioxide in the atmosphere. Currently the Paris Agreement (a political agreement) on climate change recommends that to keep global temperature rise this century well below 2 degrees Celsius, we must reduce CO_2 and other greenhouse gas emissions to 'net zero' by 2050. Under current UK emissions, Britain will use up its 2 degrees carbon budget in under nine years. Scientists disagree with the politicians – and we Green

New Dealers respect their conclusions. They argue for more urgent action – to limit warming to, at the most, 1.5 degrees by 2030. That would wipe out 90 per cent of coral reefs, and accelerate climate impacts such as wildfires, heat waves and hurricanes – but, hey, we might just survive. We could be more ambitious. Assuming the world pumped out about 42 billion tonnes (or 'gigatonnes/GTs') of CO_2 in 2018, we would have to cut 6Gt every year – roughly equivalent to the entirety of US emissions in 2009 – to hit zero by 2025. As Hazel Healy argues, there are only two ways to do this: ramping up clean energy generation while simultaneously massively reducing the fossil fuel energy we use.[5]

To achieve radical reductions our finance minister may have to consider rationing carbon. As Kevin Anderson has argued (in private conversation), if we were all starving, we would ration the food accordingly. We wouldn't give it to one small group and allow them to eat everything. So why are we acting the way we are with carbon? Carbon rationing would require trust and visible policing, as rationing did in Britain during the Second World War. Even with black market wheeling-and-dealing, with the rich trying to game the system, rationing had wide public support. With some trading and a tightening carbon budget, many people would actually be better off – as some non-combatants were during the Second World War.

Once we have resolved these issues at both international and national levels; once the annual carbon budget is calculated and agreed, the next task for the finance minister will be to make an assessment of the economy's potential.

The Economy's Capacity

The economy's potential is important, because inflation, which alters the value of money, is always a result of economic activity exceeding the capacity of the economy. In previous eras the finance sector played a major role in stoking and expanding activity, using reckless credit creation to drive production and consumption beyond safe, sustainable levels of activity, and causing inflation. A Green New Deal finance minister will order the treasury and central bank to manage credit creation to ensure it is both financially and ecologically sustainable.

Of one thing we can be confident: the careful transition to a full employment economy will not be inflationary. We know that from past experience. The Second World War proved to both the Americans and the British that everyone – even women! – could be employed without boosting inflation. The post-war Bretton Woods era was one of full employment and low inflation – until, that is, credit deregulation from the 1960s onwards began to inflate prices, as explained in my book, *The Production of Money*.[6] By 1956, post-war inflation had peaked at 7 per cent. But for most of the Bretton Woods years it remained subdued, even turning negative at the end of the 1950s. The pressures brought on by the Korean and Vietnam wars led to President Nixon's unilateral decision to dismantle the Bretton Woods international financial architecture in 1961. No system was devised to replace it. This failure enabled Wall Street and the City of London to begin attacking the system of capital controls by opening up the Eurodollar market in the late 60s. Deregulation gradually led to a rise in credit creation, which led in turn to a rise in inflation. In 1971, after 'Competition and Credit Control' ('all competition and no control') was put in place under Britain's Conservative chancellor, Anthony Barber, inflation took off in the UK. In September 1971 it had risen by almost 10 per cent. By August 1975, it had rocketed to 27 per cent.[7]

In the United States, New Deal regulation had ensured that between the Great Depression and the 1960s banking was held in check, finance was tightly moored to the real economy, and inflation was low.[8] Gradually, through the 1960s, securitisation, the lifting of Regulation Q – which capped the interest banks could offer to savers – and the recycling of petrodollars led to the earnings of Wall Street banks growing by 15 per cent a year. Inflation was the consequence, and ordinary punters were the victims.

And as so often happens, the victims were blamed. Astonishingly, economists and commentators on both the left and right of the political spectrum blame Keynes's commitment to full employment and the power of the working class – not deregulation of the international financial system – for inflationary pressures. Ignoring the fact that a deregulated finance sector is susceptible to periodic crises and is a cause of imbalances in the economy, even some Marxists are willing to blame the working class for the deregulated finance sector's role in fuelling 1970s inflation.

To prevent inflation and in order to manage the transition to full employment, a GND finance minister must ensure that capital mobility is managed, credit creation is regulated and the finance sector is tightly moored to the real economy.

Calculating Economic Capacity

To add up and calculate economic capacity is hard. One reason for this is because an economy is never static. There is continuous change, thanks to deaths and births, depreciation and production, as well as changes to the 'stocks' of people and of capital (artefacts). Another difficulty in calculating an economy's capacity is that it cannot be counted in market prices. While market prices measure the scarcity of individual goods or services relative to each other, they do not measure the *absolute* scarcity of resources in general.

The economy's capacity, once measured and calculated, can crudely be compared to a cake – albeit one that is never static. An economy at full capacity is like a plumped-up Victoria sponge. A contracting economy can be thought of as a flattened, diminished cake.

There are reasons the size of the cake matters. The first is to do with the size of the economy relative to the ecosystem within which it exists. Any sub-entity of the ecosystem must have regard to limits and boundaries. So, keeping the 'cake's' size stable relative to the ecosystem will be vital.

The second reason arises because levels of borrowing, or debt, should always be measured relative to the overall income of the economy. If the economic 'cake' shrinks, and unemployment rises, then income (including government income) contracts. The result is that (even without a rise in borrowing) the proportion owed in debt *expands* as a share of the economy. The rise in public debt after the Financial Crisis of 2007–09 was clear evidence of that phenomenon. The economy collapsed as a result of globalised financial speculation. Tax revenues slumped, causing the economic 'cake' to shrink. Automatically, as the cake shrank, public debt as a share of national income expanded, even before governments began to borrow and spend.

If there is sufficient capacity – as in large numbers of idle people and equipment, available for employment – and if there is much to do, the finance minister could safely raise (borrow) the finance needed to expand employment. The finance would be used to invest in projects that address decarbonisation challenges. As well as transforming the economy, such investment would raise incomes, not just for the employed, but also for the government in the form of tax revenues. Under those circumstances the economy would achieve balance and the debt would be more sustainable.

However, economists are notoriously bad at calculating economic capacity accurately. Since the Global Financial Crisis, many orthodox economists have claimed that economies, including many in the European Union, are at full capacity. That is to say the human and other resources of these nations are treated as fully employed, or used up. Because of this assessment, orthodox economists oppose borrowing and public investment for the creation of jobs, the revival of economic activity and for raising national income. Many advocate austerity as the alternative, fearing that expanding economic activity might lead to inflation.

Austerity has driven down wages and prices, deflated the economy and, as has already been noted, automatically increased public debt as a share of the 'shrunken cake'.

I mention this for one reason only. In the next section we will propose that our finance minister 'can afford what she can do'. Thanks to the development of monetary systems and their careful regulation, it is entirely possible to raise the finance needed to invest in the transformation of the economy away from fossil fuels. But as I shall also explain: all new money originates (via central as well as commercial banks) as credit or debt. Given the complexities and inter-dependencies of the real-world economy, maintaining full employment should ensure that debt levels do not rise and that public finances are stable. But this is more of an art than a science, even while public spending is fundamental to economic, social and political stability – and to the Green New Deal.

If we are to undertake the ambitious challenges of the Green New Deal – education and healthcare for all and an economy based on renewable energy and sustainable public transport – then we are going to have to raise large sums of money to invest in these sectors, specifically in projects that create economic activity, and especially employment. By spending and investing in jobs, governments will generate tax revenue, reduce welfare costs, and cut government debt into the bargain. Our finance minister's government can spend away the debt on a range of projects: flood defences, renewable energy, energy efficiency, social care, education, the arts, housing and transport. By investing in green-collar jobs that can't be done abroad, government spending will pay for itself, fill the economic crater caused by any fall in private investment, and lead to a recovery in the public finances. And as Herman Daly explained, the policy of limiting 'matter–energy throughput' would raise the price of energy relative to the price of labour:

> This would lead to the substitution of labour for energy in production processes and consumption patterns, thus reversing the historical trend of replacing labour with machines and inanimate energy, whose relative prices have been declining.[9]

How to Finance the GND:
Monetary and Fiscal Coordination

A key principle of the Green New Deal is that monetary and fiscal institutions work together, both to ensure the availability of finance for countering the extreme crisis we face and to maintain stability of the public finances. We wish to see monetary and fiscal institutions – the central bank and the finance ministry/treasury – working in tandem, without one or the other being dominant. In most OECD economies, fiscal and monetary policy presently work against each other. Central banks provide finance to big private financial institutions while using monetary policy to help keep government borrowing costs low. But governments are not benefitting from low rates, because fiscal policy is 'conservative' and not playing the vital role of investing at a time the private sector is too indebted and too timid to invest. So we have the extraordinary irony of indebted governments having borrowed money when rates were high, now refusing to borrow to invest in well-paid employment when interest rates are low and effectively negative. (When rates are negative, lenders are willing *to pay* borrowers to borrow. It may be hard to get one's head around that one, an exceptionally bizarre development in the weird world of today's monetary radicalism and fiscal conservatism.)

Once monetary and fiscal policy become mutually supportive, we can assume that, as in a war situation, there will be four sources of finance for a Green New Deal government. Broadly defined they can be categorised as *credit* (created anew by banks) or *savings* (such as deposits, a consequence of credit creation, and already in existence).

The first source of finance for a government is monetary credit creation (the provision of loan or overdraft facilities by the Bank of England or even by a commercial bank). The second is loan-finance, raised from *existing* savings through the issuance of gilts/bonds by the treasury and debt management office. The third source is tax revenues – with the proviso that tax revenues are generally *the consequence* of public investment and spending, not the source of finance. Fourth, a Green New Deal government could draw on the surplus resources of savers by guaranteeing bonds issued via a national investment bank/green investment bank and so on.

In the case of monetary credit creation, the government *adds* money to the stock already held by the public, in the hope that it will end up as private bank deposits, feeding back into the economy. With debt financing, *no new money is created*, instead the government draws on the existing money stock. By taxation, the government *withdraws* money from the system, and, if used to pay interest on debt, returns that money to the public (via pension funds, insurance companies, and so on) by way of payments on gilts or bonds.

It is preferable for all government spending to be

loan-financed in the first instance. The central bank may assist that process and use monetary credit creation to purchase government bonds *from the market*, and by its involvement raise the price of bonds and lower the yield. Indeed since the Great Financial Crisis the Bank of England has used its powers to purchase £435 billion of current gilts now held on its balance sheet. This approach uses asset purchases from the market to make monetary credit creation transparent. I find that far preferable to outright monetary financing of government spending.

To kick-start the process, various government departments will prepare programmes or projects, calculate the cost of these programmes and submit bids to the finance minister.

The loan-finance can then be raised by the government treasury or by a national investment bank. These institutions will issue bonds – equivalent to the finance needed to pay for government programmes. Those bonds will likely be bought by those with savings (public and private) pension funds and insurance companies, entities that need to invest in safe assets that offer a return so that future pensions, etc., can be paid. In a process that is essentially cyclical, while governments will pay interest on finance borrowed from pension funds, the revenues from those interest payments will, as noted above, one day return to taxpayers in the form of pension payments. Depending on circumstances, government bonds may also be purchased (or financed) by the nation's or the region's central bank. In that case, government bonds will be paid for with central bank reserves or deposits. The central bank's role will be to buy sufficient bonds to ensure that the yield on government bonds remains low, to ensure sustainability of repayment.

As is now well understood, central bankers (like licensed commercial bankers) have the power to create new central bank money (deposits), known as reserves, 'out of thin air'. They have enjoyed this power for centuries. In the past their ability to create new deposits was referred to as Open Market Operations (OMOs). More recently the moniker Quantitative Easing has been attached to the practice of OMOs, as the quantity of operations was projected to expand. The experience of post-2008 bailouts demonstrated that central bankers have the power to issue vast sums of emergency finance overnight. Earth systems breakdown is hardly less of an emergency.

That finance, made available to governments by the central bank as loan-finance, can then be spent into the economy by different government departments – just as loan-finance from commercial banks can be spent into the economy by firms and individuals.

Tax revenues will be collected and used to balance the books and pay down the borrowing costs. Tax *policy* can be used to increase the cost of carbon for the 10 per cent of emitters that the economists Chancel and Piketty show are responsible for close to 50 per cent of emissions.[10] As Professor Kevin Anderson has argued, acknowledging that emissions are highly skewed towards a relatively small proportion of the population is a prerequisite of any meaningful fiscal policy.[11] But, as we explained in Chapter 4, taxation of the rest of society who emit far less than the top 10 per cent will have to take distributive effects into account, and would best be deployed *after* investment in renewable energy and sustainable transport is front-loaded to provide citizens with alternatives.

Balancing Interest

Central bankers have the power to influence interest rates, and to lower them quickly and dramatically as needs be. Many orthodox economists, supported by progressive 'green' economists, argue for high rates of interest as a way of curbing excessive credit creation. But experience has taught that high interest rates are not a deterrent to borrowing. One has only to think of the sub-prime crisis, caused by risky borrowers borrowing at very high, real rates of interest. It is more important for central banks to tighten the *regulation* of credit creation, to ensure that credit is created for productive, income-generating activity, and not speculation, and that rates remain low. This is because low rates of interest are vital to the sustainability of green finance. This echoes Keynes, who argued that tight but cheap credit is far preferable to easy but dear credit. That is why, after 2008, central bankers cut interest rates to bail out the private financial system and to assist the public sector to cope with the crisis. In moves that were historically unprecedented, central bank rates were reduced into negative territory. Never in monetary history have rates been as low.

Central bankers then used what is known as 'forward guidance' to manage rates of interest applied by banks and other financial institutions to those active in the real economy. While central bank rates were depressed, *they were made available only to financial institutions*. Rates in the real, non-financial economy are not low in real terms (i.e., relative to deflationary pressures). A striking example of the *real rate of interest* applied to the non-financial economy was revealed when British Steel was forced into compulsory liquidation in 2019. Three years earlier, British Steel had been acquired by what is in effect a private equity firm, Greybull. Frances Coppola explains what happened next:

> In May 2016, Greybull, via an opaque company called Olympus Steel registered in the British tax haven of Jersey, advanced British Steel £154m ($195m) at an interest rate of 9% over six-month sterling Libor. Sterling Libor is currently just under 1%, so the effective interest rate on the loan is nearly 10%. British Steel also has loans from banks at 3% over sterling Libor. The company's owner is extracting cash at a rate 6% higher than that charged by banks.

For companies to generate returns of 9 per cent per annum, or even on the lower interest rate of 4 per cent, requires profits to exceed those levels. For profits to exceed those levels requires the extraction of additional value from the company's labour force, from its capital stock and ultimately from the ecosystem. It should come as no surprise that British Steel was unable to extract such high rates of return – or that such high extractive rates have caused immeasurable harm to the ecosystem.

After the prolonged eurozone crisis, the European Central Bank (ECB) introduced a refinancing operation known as 'targeted long-term refinancing operations', or TLTROs. As a result of that operation, commercial banks were able to borrow from the ECB at the deposit rate (*minus* 0.4 per cent), provided the money was lent on to companies active in the real economy. Low levels of European investment are a strong indication that the money was not lent on. Bankers took the cheap finance – and no doubt used it for speculation in the shadow banking sector.

Under the Green New Deal, the great powers of publicly backed central bankers will no longer be used almost exclusively for private sector speculation and enrichment. They will be deployed instead to finance productive investment, at low rates of interest, in the transformation of the economy away from fossil fuels.

Against Modern Monetary Theory

'Green QE' and MMT are areas of monetary policy over which there is much controversy. The British Green New Deal group is divided over these issues. I am opposed to what can be regarded as one-sided monetary schemes, sometimes defined as 'deficit financing'. (The term, by the way, is an oxymoron, as deficits are the budgeted *outcome* of spending and investment, not a source of finance.)

Since the Great Financial Crisis of 2007–09 there has been an increasingly vociferous chorus of demands for 'Green QE' or 'People's QE.' These calls have been amplified by a campaign for a fixed set of policies defined as Modern Monetary Theory (MMT).

It is not hard to understand why these demands have arisen. They are a reaction to the policy of 'monetary radicalism and fiscal conservatism' launched in 2009 by a candidate for British prime minister, David Cameron. He ushered in 'The Age of Austerity' by making great play of the fact that he was a 'monetary radical and fiscal conservative'.[12]

Since 2009, the world's four biggest central banks – the European Central Bank, the Bank of Japan, the Bank of England and the United States Federal Reserve – have embraced 'monetary radicalism'. They have drastically lowered interest rates and pumped around $13–20 trillion into the global economy. In addition to this largesse, both the ECB and the Bank of England have provided generous subsidies to the private banking sector. Nevertheless, and despite low, even negative rates and an enormous, unprecedented injection of liquidity, central bankers have failed to revive the global economy. Despite considerable effort on that front, they have conspicuously failed to raise inflation above 2 per cent in both Europe and the United States. Indeed, deflationary pressures have this year once again reared their ugly head. (Deflation lowers prices and wages, but also profits, leading to falls in investment and employment. It also automatically increases the cost of debt.)

This central bank failure was largely the fault of economists' prescriptions for austerity: for the policy of 'monetary radicalism and fiscal conservatism'. It is a policy that has proved a costly failure. As is now well understood, central banks cannot do all the heavy lifting alone. Instead, and predictably, QE simply served to inflate the value of assets. And as assets are owned by the already wealthy, QE exacerbated the already obscene levels of global inequality.

It is *that* failure that has fuelled calls for 'Green QE' or 'People's QE', and it also, to an extent, underpins Modern Monetary Theory – in response to the perception that central bank financing has mainly benefitted a privileged elite of financiers, while the majority of the population suffers under 'austerity'.

'Green QE 'or 'People's QE' and MMT all assume that

central banks can, and should, effectively print money for direct distribution to citizens or for direct financing of government spending. I disagree.

The first objection arises from the nature of money or credit creation in the first place. The actual 'production' of bank credit-money arises out of *nothing more than the promise of repayment*, as Joseph Schumpeter once explained. Both central bank and commercial bank money originates as credit or debt. There is no such thing as debt-free money. Debt-free money is a gift or a grant of *existing* savings, it is not new money.

The 'promise to pay' (made by an individual, a firm or a government) is underwritten by the offer of collateral as guarantee of repayment, the signing of a contract that promises to repay, and the agreement to a rate of interest on the loan. Only then can a commercial bank or central bank use their extraordinary powers to deposit new money (which is always and everywhere credit) in the borrower's account.

QE involves the exchange of assets and liabilities between the bank and its clients. Both central and commercial banks create credit 'out of thin air' but *always* in exchange for collateral, a contract and a rate of interest fixed over a time period. The creation of debt-free money – money created without a) the exchange of deposits for collateral, b) a contract promising to repay, at c) a certain rate of interest, over d) a given period of time – would not be QE. It would not even be money, as understood by all those that use money.

By borrowing money, that is, by issuing bonds into markets, governments raise finance and make public their financing requirements. Bonds (gilts or treasury bills) are backed by, say, Britain's 30 million taxpayers or by the United States' 60 million taxpayers. As a consequence of that backing, bonds are certainly *liabilities* for the government (in the sense that the bond has to be repaid at interest), but they are simultaneously valuable *assets* for exchange with the central bank, and for those who may wish to purchase the asset (and its annual interest payments) by lending to the government.

Markets provide a level of transparency to the process of government borrowing. As someone who has worked extensively in Africa on the issue of sovereign debt, I am only too aware of the possibility and danger of collusion between politicians and central bank bureaucracies. African governments are not alone. Donald Trump's efforts to discredit the Federal Reserve by packing the board with right-wing extremists wilfully undermines the integrity of a public institution that should be answerable to all Americans, not just the far right. Transparent transactions in the marketplace shine a light on government borrowing intentions, and on the actions of central bank civil servants, and are thereby accountable to all citizens.

To support government borrowing, central banks can transparently intervene in bond markets, and can purchase government bonds for new finance. By so doing the central bank can lower the yield on that borrowing. They do this by purchasing and removing bonds or treasury bills from the market. This makes much-sought-after sovereign bonds scarce, which raises the price of the remaining bonds. Because of the way bonds work, the higher price lowers the yield (roughly, the rate of interest) on government bonds.

Modern Monetary Theorists and 'Green QE' advocates hope to bypass this process. Instead of elected government ministers in the driver's seat deciding on a government's financing needs by issuing bonds into transparent markets, Modern Monetary Theorists (MMTers) would permit civil servants and technocrats in central banks to determine and issue quantities of what campaigners call 'new money' into the economy – behind closed doors. This would, in my view, bestow excessive powers on technocratic civil servants whose record in managing the monetary system has been somewhat blemished by the financial crisis. The transfer of such powers to the central bank and away from the political process lacks transparency and would be detrimental to regulatory democracy.

Disagreement over 'Peoples QE' and MMT arises also over the inflationary impact. While it is true that central banks have enormous powers to issue liquidity, those powers must be managed and regulated, for two reasons. First, for accountability purposes and second, to manage inflation. Because of 'monetary radicalism', central bankers have had a free pass to issue vast amounts of liquidity to their asset-holding clients – mainly banks and financial institutions. This has fuelled a huge inflation of asset prices and caused distortions to the economy, while also exacerbating inequality and inciting public anger. Because the rich and powerful are the beneficiaries of asset price inflation, it has not been as controversial as price and wage inflation would have been. But it is just as distortionary as consumer price inflation.

The dominance of monetary policy after the Financial Crisis led to the colossal expansion of QE aimed largely at the private finance sector, not at governments, which (for ideological reasons) restrained their borrowing. Cuts in government borrowing and spending – austerity – led ultimately to a shortage of the world's safest and most sought-after assets – the sovereign bonds of OECD countries. Pension funds, asset management funds and insurance funds need to earn interest on their investments to build up resources for paying pensions and insurance in the future. Given the shortage of sovereign debt, pension and other funds poured their savings into riskier assets. These include the bonds of countries like Turkey and Brazil, where, because of economic instability, rates of interest are much higher. This diversion away from safe British and European bonds and into riskier assets poses a threat to future pensioners, and could be the source of a future crisis.

The post-2008 experience revealed why a one-sided financial system, dependent largely on central bank money, worsens imbalances and global inequality. Those imbalances include government deficits, as low tax revenues made it hard for governments to balance their books. MMTers dispute this, arguing that tax revenues can be used to fight inflation (i.e. withdraw income from the economy) or for distributional purposes, but are not important for balancing the government's accounts. That is because, in their view, governments can just print money to balance their books. Indeed, MMTers seem to celebrate, and make a virtue of deficits and debt.

I disagree, strongly. The creation of credit and therefore debt is an extraordinarily valuable development. One has only to think of poor countries that lack sound monetary systems and the institutions that underpin a monetary system (an independent central bank, criminal justice systems for enforcing contracts, accounting systems and a sound tax collection system) to understand why poor countries lack money – and have to depend on richer countries for funds. Still, while a sound monetary system and the ability of both central and commercial banks to create credit effortlessly is vital, imbalances caused by excessive and speculative credit creation leads to high levels of deficits and debt. These, as we know from current experience, are impoverishing of individuals and extractive of the ecosystem, as well as systemically destabilising.

Tax revenues, derived from public and private spending financed by loans, are essential for a 'steady state' monetary system that avoids the build-up of debt and deficits – in other words, imbalances in the system. While governments may incur debt by borrowing, that borrowing must be spent wisely on employment that will generate tax revenues for the repayment of public debt, to keep the system in relative balance.

Finally, 'money-printing' will have distributional effects – £600 paid direct into bank accounts (argue 'People's QE' advocates) will have a big impact on a poor woman's budget, but is a generous gift to the wealthy who do not need it. For fair distributive purposes, these effects are best managed by political decisions via the system of taxation, not the monetary system.

There is one more important reason why Modern Monetary Theory is flawed. Most MMTers are based in the United States. They live and work in an economy based on the dollar, which thanks to America's imperial power, serves as the world's reserve currency. The US, unlike other sovereigns, can use the 'exorbitant privilege' bestowed on the global reserve currency to purchase most goods and services its citizens need from anywhere on earth. Like the privileges enjoyed by the banker in a game of monopoly, there is almost no limit to the money the US can 'print' for those purchases, and therefore almost no limit to US consumption of the world's goods and services. Because the United States is monetarily sovereign, it does not need to finance purchases in any currency other than its own. That is not true for the rest of the world – especially poor countries that cannot purchase oil, gas and finished goods in their own currency. Instead they are obliged to pay for these vital goods using a foreign currency, invariably the dollar. For all countries except the US, there are severe limits to sovereignty.

To conclude: a well-managed monetary system can, with the support of the central bank, ensure the provision of both publicly and privately sourced loan-finance at low, sustainable or even zero rates of interest, for public and private projects that are sound, not speculative. In a circular process that maintains stability and balance, tax revenues are raised as a consequence of central and commercial bank financing of investment in economic activity, mainly employment. Most of the investment goes into the creation of new assets, for example, the building of flood defences, the education of children or the development of musical skills. A proportion of the balance can be used to repay debts, including public debt, to keep the nation's accounts in balance.

Savings

Under the programme outlined above, savings are not needed for investment. Nevertheless, and in part due to central bank credit-creation, there are staggering quantities of savings stashed away in both public and private pension funds, asset management funds, insurance companies, sovereign wealth funds and other financial institutions. So credit-creation need not be the only source of financing for our putative finance minister. She could choose to actively intervene to mobilise the public's existing savings, currently managed by private institutional funds. Consideration should be given to the nationalisation of institutions that manage the savings of millions of citizens, so that their resources could be aimed at decarbonisation projects to benefit future pensioners.

To gain some idea of the quantity of the world's savings, we have data collected by the Financial Stability Board (FSB), set up by the G20 to monitor the global financial system following the crisis. The FSB estimates that overall, total global financial assets of all financial corporations grew by 5.3 per cent in 2017, to reach $382.3 trillion in forty jurisdictions.[13] OECD pension funds held savings valued at about $43 trillion in 2017.[14] Shadow banking assets amounted to $185 trillion. Norway holds the biggest sovereign wealth fund in the world, estimated at $872 billion. This vast quantity of savings must be compared to global GDP in current prices, which, according to the World Bank, amounted to only $80.7 trillion in 2017.[15]

We can therefore safely conclude that there are potential supplies of both public and private *credit* for the purposes of saving the planet and, secondly, there are staggeringly large supplies of both public and private *savings* that could be released to the same end.

Costing a Global Green New Deal

The future is unknown and so calculations around future costs will always be subject to substantial margins of error. Also the impact on the poor arising from the emissions of the wealthy is underestimated in all global costings of earth systems breakdown. As Kevin Anderson explains,

> Cut away the economic niceties and the social cost of carbon is little more than an attempt by a particular hue of economists to put a price on the global scale impacts of climate change, from now, throughout this century, and on across centuries to come. Such hubris is the preserve of a select group of typically wealthy, white and high-emitting men in the Northern hemisphere. Sat behind computers in highly industrialised countries, they price the impact of their and our carbon-profligacy on poor, low-emitting, climate-vulnerable, and geographically distant communities. A dollar value is put on the devastation a strengthened tornado wreaks on small coastal towns, financially valuing the people killed, the destroyed homes and destitute neighbourhoods.[16]

With these caveats we can make a start, if only to show the affordability of transformation. To begin with, we draw on the work of experts at the IMF and the Global Commission on the Economy and Climate.[17] The IMF has reviewed business-as-usual infrastructure investment already in the pipeline. It has estimated that the world is expected to invest around US$90 trillion in infrastructure over the next fifteen years. The worrying part of their estimate is that the world is planning to use $90 trillion to *double* today's entire current stock of infrastructure, without due regard to the 'carrying capacity' of the ecosystem. The purpose will be to replace ageing infrastructure and to 'accommodate structural change in emerging and developing economies'. This will require, explains the IMF, a doubling of annual global investment in infrastructure, from $3.4 trillion to about $6 trillion each year.

The Global Commission on the Economy and Climate has found that 'it does not need to cost much more to ensure that this new infrastructure is compatible with climate goals, and the additional up-front costs can be fully offset by efficiency gains and fuel savings over the infrastructure lifecycle.'[18]

In other words, experts have calculated that $90 trillion of financing, spent over the next fifteen years at a rate of about $6 trillion per annum, is already in the pipeline. The Global Commission on the Economy and Climate believe these sums would cover infrastructure investment 'compatible with climate goals'. Given that hundreds of billions of dollars could be saved if public subsidies were withdrawn from fossil fuels, that indicates that roughly $7 trillion per annum can be earmarked for investment in transformative infrastructure. $7 trillion is roughly 8.75 per cent of global income (GDP). That sum could double and still only amount to 18 per cent of global GDP.

The figure of $7 trillion per annum invested in economic and ecological transformation may well be insufficient, but it would amount to fully $10 trillion *less* than estimates of global inaction.

A recent article in the journal *Nature* calculated the cumulative economic impact caused by each tonne of pollutant sent into the atmosphere.[19] China and the United States, the world's two largest emitters of carbon dioxide, will be hit with the highest social costs, according to the scientists. The impact on China will be $24 per tonne of carbon and on the US $48 per tonne. Combined country-level costs, according to this study, amount to more than $400 in social costs per tonne of CO_2. Based on CO_2 emissions in 2017, that's a global and annual impact of more than $16 trillion.

In 2017, disasters triggered by weather- and climate-related hazards led to global losses of US$320 billion. Devastating floods in South Asia took more than 1,200 lives, while communities in the Caribbean are still struggling to recover from the unprecedented hurricane season.[20] For 2018, the insurance giant AON estimated global economic costs of extreme weather at $215 billion in the wake of hundreds of cyclones, floods and wildfires. Rival insurer Munich Re set the bill for extreme weather in 2018 at $160 billion. AON suggests that 2017–18 was the costliest two-year period on record for extreme weather disasters, reaching $653 billion.[21]

Added to these costs are the subsidies and tax breaks that

the finance ministry of our model country provides to private fossil fuel-extracting corporations. The IMF estimates that

> globally, subsidies remained large at $4.7 trillion (6.3 percent of global GDP) in 2015 and are projected at $5.2 trillion (6.5 percent of GDP) in 2017. The largest subsidizers in 2015 were China ($1.4 trillion), United States ($649 billion), Russia ($551 billion), European Union ($289 billion), and India ($209 billion). About three-quarters of global subsidies are due to domestic factors – energy pricing reform thus remains largely in countries' own national interest – while coal and petroleum together account for 85 percent of global subsidies. Efficient fossil fuel pricing in 2015 would have lowered global carbon emissions by 28 percent and fossil fuel air pollution deaths by 46 percent, and increased government revenue by 3.8 percent of GDP.[22]

Some of these costs may overlap. Most of the reckoning in human lives and livelihoods and in ecosystem damage are uncountable. Nevertheless, we can reliably state that conservative estimates of the annual social costs of inaction amount to roughly $22 trillion – more than 25 per cent of global income.

There is an added potential cost. If fossil fuel companies continue to hedge their bets, by taking action too slowly and with mixed signals to the market, that could culminate, according to the Commission, in $12 trillion of stranded fossil fuel assets by 2035.[23] By comparison the bailout for stranded mortgage assets, which triggered the 2008 financial crisis, was a mere $250 billion.

Our finance minister would have to calculate her government's share of these costs and subsidies. They are likely to be very high. Still, as any strategy for decarbonisation will have to consider the removal of subsidies to the fossil fuel sector, there will be considerable savings put at her disposal by suspending these subsidies.

Therefore, a Green New Deal finance minister should act strategically and, as explained in Chapter 4, should aim carbon taxes at the biggest emitters. They have been free-riding on the global economy for too long – and by not internalising their costs are evidence of the biggest market failure of all. As a guide for our finance minister, the Climate Disclosure Project has helpfully listed the highest emitting companies since 1988 that are investor-owned.[24] They include: ExxonMobil, Shell, BP, Chevron, Peabody, Total, and BHP Billiton. Key state-owned companies include Saudi Aramco, Gazprom, National Iranian Oil, Coal India, Pemex and CNPC (PetroChina). Coal emissions from China are represented by the state, in which key state-owned producers include Shenhua Group, Datong Coal Mine Group and China National Coal Group. These companies, and not low-emitting individuals, should play a pivotal role in the global energy transition.

One of the most harmful sectors is the airline industry, and it is wrong that no excise duty is paid on aviation fuel across the European Union (although it is in the US,

Australia, Japan, Canada and Saudi Arabia), and VAT is not charged on airline ticket sales. Indeed it ought to be a priority for a Green New Deal government to curtail the activities of both the airline and shipping industries – major contributors to the build-up of carbon emissions.

At the same time our finance minister's government should frontload investment in extreme-weather-event protection to build resilience; alternative surface transport; the power sector; improvements to building insulation; and in agriculture and land use, by reforesting and sequestering carbon in soils, peatlands and salt marshes. Only then should taxes be applied to change behaviours.

When the Mayor of London announced that he was going to introduce a tax on all drivers in the city in 2003 – a 'congestion charge' – there was uproar. Among those opposed were his own left-wing supporters. On the day the congestion charge was introduced, 300 extra buses were added to the central London network. Mayor Livingstone had, while planning what was effectively a carbon tax, simultaneously invested in a massive expansion of buses and bus routes in London. One year later, 29,000 more passengers were entering London by bus during the morning rush hour.[25] And so the congestion charge was quickly accepted by the public, and has proved successful by reducing traffic and congestion and allowing road space to be given over to pedestrians and cyclists. In short, carbon taxes on the wider population should be considered only *after* alternative systems have been made available.

◄►

Our monetary system and vast quantities of global savings make financing the transformation of the economy away from fossil fuels eminently affordable. The real challenge to be faced by Green New Dealers will be to ensure that carbon budgets are rigorously based on science and are radically cut back each year to ensure the ultimate survival of humanity. Second, equity must be at the heart of all economic, ecological and political decision-making. That is the hard part of budgeting. Compared to that, and given the monetary and fiscal tools available to a finance minister, financial budgeting will not be quite as challenging.

6

The Green New Deal: Transforming Our World

We live in capitalism. Its power seems inescapable. So did the divine right of kings. Any human power can be resisted and changed by human beings. Resistance and change often begin in art, and very often in our art, the art of words.

Ursula K. Le Guin

It was just a montage of words uttered over a video in the summer of 2018; soon the words went viral. They helped unseat a Wall Street–friendly Democrat, one primed to be the next Congressional leader. They were uttered by Alexandria Ocasio-Cortez: 'This race is about people vs money. We've got people. They've got money. A New York for the many *is* possible. It doesn't take a hundred years to do this. It takes political courage.'

She was right. It did not take a hundred years. All it took was one summer, plus political courage, a big idea – The Green New Deal – and hard graft. A Green New Deal sets out to subordinate the financial system to the interests of society and the ecosystem, and help transform the economy away from its addiction to fossil fuels, AOC announced. The big idea, her hard work and her courage were all that was needed to harness a latent power: the power of the people of the Bronx.

But how is this extraordinary programme to be achieved? A first in the many steps that must be taken if we are to harness the latent power of people is to spread public understanding. People cannot act to transform that which they do not understand.

So, to begin: one of the most important facts to understand is this. Taxpaying citizens have immense, potential power. Millions of honest, law-abiding taxpayers help to uphold the economic system and provide public services by regularly paying their taxes. But they do more. Their taxes also guarantee and endorse the activities of the globalised, deregulated private financial sector. Private financial markets cannot function *without* the backing of governments, their taxpayers, and the safety of public debt. In the words of Mariana Mazzucato, the 'timid mouse' that is the globalised private finance sector cannot operate without the protection of the 'roaring lion' that is the public sector.[1]

Carefully invested taxpayer-backed public borrowing, or public debt, is not only of great value in creating good jobs and essential infrastructure. It is also of immense importance to the private, globalised 'shadow banking' sector in generating income, and leveraging additional finance. While guilt, sin and the public debt are deeply intertwined in the minds of economists, journalists and the public, it becomes something quite different in the minds of financiers and rentiers. To Wall Street and the City of London, the safe public debt of Britain, Europe and the US is a truly awesome and even phenomenal gift. They cannot get enough of it.

Until we fully grasp the importance of public debt to the finance sector, then we will lack the ability to leverage power over immensely wealthy, globalised corporations and individuals. If we turn a blind eye to the value they attach to our taxes and government debts, then they will continue to parasitically extract rent from public assets, and we will become relatively poorer and more powerless.

There is another aspect to safe, public collateral not widely understood. Namely, how it is used in the shadow banking system – the private financial system that operates in the financial 'stratosphere', beyond the reach of states and regulatory democracy. Non-regulated bank-like entities that have scooped up the world's savings (such as asset management funds, pension funds and insurance companies) hold vast quantities of cash. BlackRock, for example, holds about $6 trillion in financial assets. These sums cannot safely be deposited in a traditional bank, where only a limited amount is guaranteed by governments. So, to protect the value of the cash, the asset management fund will, for example, make a temporary loan of *cash* to another that needs it, in exchange for, or guaranteed by, collateral. This exchange is known as a 'repo', or repurchase arrangement.

As Daniela Gabor has argued, the US and European repo markets, the largest in the world, are built on valuable collateral: government debt. In her words, 'the state has become a collateral factory for shadow banking.'[2] The risks of this unregulated market for the global financial system are scary. One reason is that while someone operating in the real world, say a homeowner, may only once be able to re-mortgage her asset or property, unregulated shadow bankers can use a single unit of collateral to re-leverage a number of times. Manmohan Singh of the IMF has estimated that, by late 2007, the same collateral 'churned' or was used roughly three times to leverage additional borrowing in speculative markets.[3] That's like using the value of a single asset — one's property — to guarantee additional borrowing from three different banks.

To harness citizens' power behind the transformation of the global economy, it is important to understand that taxpayers have agency over global financial markets. Around the world, taxpayers subsidise, embolden and enrich centres of financial power like Wall Street and the City of London. The bank bailouts after the 2008 crisis demonstrated that citizens and their publicly financed institutions are equipped to protect capitalism's rentiers from the discipline of the 'free market'. Thanks to the backing and firepower provided by millions of honest, taxpaying citizens, central banks deployed their immense financial might and bailed out the globalised banking system – stemming a cascade of debt deleveraging that could have contracted the money supply, credit, and economic activity and deepened the crisis further. Thanks to taxpayers, central bankers prevented another Great Depression. It was a great power deployed in the name of citizens, but without their authority – or even their knowledge.

This power lies in abeyance, suppressed by the dominant moneyed class. But suppressed also by the narrow, myopic view that we, and our politicians, have of the potential economic power of citizens.

To deploy this financial power in the interests of society and the planet, citizens need to understand that this was ultimately *our* latent power, which should have been used by citizens to defend the public interest, rather than by technocrats to defend the interests of private wealth.

We must now grasp that power. Only then can we begin to demand 'terms and conditions' for taxpayer-backed subsidies and guarantees – and use that power to regulate and subordinate the globalised financial sector to the interests of society as a whole. To demand that public financial assets be used for public, not private benefit, and be deployed in the service of humanity and the ecosystem.

The Possibility of Rapid Transition

Andrew Simms is one of the co-authors of the original British Green New Deal. For years he has worked on plans for a 'rapid transition'. He argues, as does Wanda Vrasti, that this is not just a crisis of systemic proportions, but also a crisis of imagination. In Vrasti's words, 'decades of being told There Is No Alternative, that liberal capitalism is the only rational way of organizing society, has atrophied our ability to imagine social forms of life that defy the bottom line.'[4]

First, we can't imagine a situation being different. Then things change, and we can't imagine going back to how they were before.[5] Those in positions to influence events are challenged to learn from previous scenarios – where, when and how things have been changed in the past. With this, a greater shared understanding of what works can be nurtured, to create action at the scale and speed needed.

As an example, the Rapid Transition Alliance offers smoking – promoted by an industry that knew all about, but publicly denied, the fact that smoking killed millions of people. Transformation in the face of those powerful corporate interests was achieved, and relatively quickly.

Today in Britain, less than one in five adults still smoke. But in the early 1970s, over half of all men and over 40 per cent of women smoked. What can we learn from the anti-smoking campaign? First, think a generation ahead – by educating and awareness-raising among young people. Next, make the product less affordable. Insist on negative branding – place images of cancer victims on cigarette packets. Regulate harmful products.[6] And so on . . .

The Rapid Transition Alliance reminds us of what happened quite recently, when a volcano – Eyjafjallajökull – erupted in the early morning of 14 April 2010. Within hours airports all over Europe were closing. The fine dust thrown up by the volcano was lethal to modern jet engines. For days Europe was grounded. One of the main arteries of the modern world – cheap, ubiquitous air travel – was suddenly severed. It was, writes Simms, as if a giant master switch for the aviation industry had been flicked to 'off'.[7] It was also a glimpse of a future in which climate breakdown and limited oil supplies will have clipped the airline industry's wings. The world did not come to a standstill. The sky didn't fall. The event revealed how life would be different without airlines: it would simply go on, as it has done for thousands of years.

When governments throw their weight behind new infrastructures, they can be rolled out at remarkable speed. State-led financing of new infrastructures has many precedents. In Britain between 1845 and 1852, 4,400 miles of railway track were laid. On a single weekend in 1892, engineers working with a perfectly coordinated army of 4,200 workers laid a total of 177 miles of track along the Great Western route to the South West of Britain, converting the old broad-gauge lines to the new standard, or narrow gauge.[8]

The New Deal's Rural Electrification Act is another key example of state-led ambition. As late as 1935, 90 per cent of American homes in rural areas had no electricity, as historian Louis Hyman explains.[9] Five years later, 40 per cent of rural America had electricity, a rise of 30 per cent in only a few years. By 1950, 90 per cent had electricity. Moreover, this example demonstrates, first, how important citizen participation and cooperation was to the New Deal, and second it shows how the 'roaring lion' of the public sector can work with the 'timid mouse' of the private sector to mutual advantage. Private utilities had baulked at the perceived expense of stringing electricity lines across miles of empty land for just a few customers. The leader of the New Deal's Rural Electrification Administration (REA), Morris Cooke, an engineer and head of Philadelphia's public works was a practical man and found a middle path between big corporations and big government. This took the form of rural cooperatives that had for years served American farmers. The REA did not manage the actual work. Instead it offered cooperatives capital and technical support, empowering Americans to get together and take control of the local economy ... Later on, these cooperatives were denounced as 'communist' by utilities, but they were anything but. Their work made possible the modernization of the American farm and farmhouse, which in turn made it possible for rural America to buy electrical goods from private companies. They also returned a modest profit.[10]

Furthermore, the Roosevelt administration demonstrated through the REA that public initiatives 'crowded in' private initiatives – and not the reverse.

Finally, the arrival of the internet and the speed with which it has brought about an extraordinary transformation in communication and information was not predicted, nor could we have imagined such change was possible in so short a time.

Our own experience tells us, then, that change can happen – and fast.

Courage and Leadership

Gordon Brown, the former British prime minister, recently warned that we survive precariously in a leaderless world. The cooperation that was seen in 2008, he wrote in the *Guardian*, would not be possible in a post-2018 crisis, in terms of central banks and governments working collaboratively.[11]

That is largely true, but Brown is wrong in one respect. There *has* been leadership and consistent international coordination since 2009. Not by politicians, but by the civil servants in charge of publicly backed central banks.

International coordination by central bankers saved the finance sector, but not the world. How are we to save the world? How do societies, democracies, wrest back control over the globalised monetary system to bring about the system change needed if we are to save the planet? We might begin by demanding that central banks change their orientation – moving away from the small elite of speculators in the globalised financial system and towards the millions of people who expect to be supported by taxpayer-backed public institutions.

Second, we must understand that, as Greta Thunberg insists, we the people are the greatest source of hope. We're not stupid or evil. We are simply not aware. Once we realise, we act. We change, and we bring about change.

I know that from my own experience. Thanks to greater awareness about the complexity and injustice of sovereign debt – awareness generated by the debt cancellation campaign, Jubilee 2000 – millions of ordinary people were empowered to take action. Their actions, coordinated across continents, demonstrated sustained international North–South solidarity, and forced powerful institutions, including the IMF and World Bank, to cancel $100 billion (in nominal terms) of the debts of thirty-five low-income countries.

People power changed the financial predicament of many of the world's most indebted countries and brought about structural changes in their relationships with the international financial institutions. So, we know it can be done.

But we need more than people power.

For change to happen, both courage and leadership will be essential. As I write this, the people of Hong Kong have assembled in their millions to challenge the extraordinary power of the Chinese government. In light of the history of Chinese protest, that takes guts. During the April 2019 Extinction Rebellion demonstrations, Farhana Yamin, an international climate lawyer and diplomat, defiantly charged through a police line and superglued her hands to the pavement outside the London HQ of oil company Shell. For a woman of her distinction and reputation, that took courage.

Yamin was not alone. Hundreds of ordinary people demonstrated courage. They sacrificed personal lives, livelihoods and relationships to endure arrest and draw attention to the fact that humanity is facing an unprecedented global emergency.

But courage and awareness are not enough. We also need leadership – organisational and political leadership.

For organisations or communities steeped in egalitarian, cooperative cultures, many baulk at the concept of leadership, but also at the opportunity to lead. It is a burden not lightly worn, because the personal costs and the price of failure are high. A woman who was my dear friend – Wangari Maathai – was a leader. She was the first woman in East Africa to earn a doctorate, and the first African woman to win the Nobel Prize.[12] She exercised leadership in her country, Kenya, by mobilising women to plant trees. She sacrificed her academic career to raise funds for the creation of tree nurseries across Kenya. By so doing she encouraged and empowered poor Kenyan women, and provided them with livelihoods from tree planting. She dug holes with them in the badly eroded, red soil of their villages – holes in which they planted hope for today and forests for tomorrow.[13] She led protests to protect Uhuru Park in Nairobi from expropriation by the corrupt President Daniel Moi, and defended the urban Karura Forest from Moi's plans for a huge real estate project. She was humiliated and attacked, received death threats and was imprisoned by Moi. But in the end, it was Wangari and the Green Belt Movement of tree-planting women that helped bring down President Moi in 2002.

Wangari was a leader. A woman who led her community in a struggle for lasting change. Unity and cohesion are often the result of effective leadership: strong, principled women and men with vision and optimism to inspire others. Leaders who are loyal to and connected with their stakeholders – their base. Leaders willing to risk unpopularity, make personal sacrifices, exercise responsibility and demonstrate integrity. Leaders who open up frontiers of both debate and action previously considered impassable. Leaders who remain true to their mandate, while acting decisively.

The truth is that for want of effective leadership, most campaigns fail.

But awareness, courage and leadership are not enough. As Frederick Douglass argued long ago,

> Power concedes nothing without a demand. It never did and it never will. Find out just what any people will quietly submit to and you have found out the exact measure of injustice and wrong which will be imposed upon them, and these will continue till they are resisted with either words or blows, or with both.[14]

Back in 2009, before the Copenhagen conference on climate change, I watched in dismay as a 'green' demonstration assembled in London's Trafalgar Square. A relatively small group of people (I had witnessed many much larger demonstrations descend on that famous square) were there to demand that world leaders do something to protect societies from climate breakdown. But it was not at all clear what exactly was wanted of those leaders. This was because neither they, nor their own leaders, had arrived at a consensus behind an 'ask' – a demand – of the rich and powerful gathered in Copenhagen.

There was no slogan for radical, structural change akin to 'women demand the vote'; 'constitutional and legal rights for African Americans'; 'cancel poor country debt by 2000' or 'repeal apartheid laws'. The reason why was plain to see. Like a football ground covered in advertising by competing brands, Trafalgar Square was covered in the banners and posters of many different non-governmental organisations – some green, some not. Despite all the 'messaging', these organisations were preoccupied with their own survival and had failed to cooperate to unite behind a single demand of world leaders. Instead they were involved in a competitive game of raising profiles to secure additional funding.

The green movement, dubbed the 'largest movement on earth', was vast and diverse, but also disunited, atomised and marginalised. Greens had largely focused on individual ('change your lightbulbs') or community ('recycle, reuse, reduce, localise') action. Many had been weak at understanding and promoting the need for radical *structural change* across sectors and at a global and national level – change that involves state action. And such structural change cannot just be undertaken at the level of international negotiations on the environment. It has to embrace, as the Green New Deal does, the need for structural change to the global financial and economic system.

That is now happening. The movement is finally beginning to coalesce at an international level behind a single demand for the structurally radical Green New Deal. It is a global banner behind which millions can assemble with one voice in order to address the gravest crisis humanity has ever faced.

In Britain, the United States and Europe, Green New Deal campaigns are building support and making specific demands of those in power. The GND has already forged unity and collaboration between progressive forces within national boundaries and deepened bonds at the international level. Campaigners need to use its key elements to mobilise a worldwide force for change. We need to get political, and to support those that engage in the brutal politics of structural change, not just behavioural change – if we are to win our demands and shift the balance of power away from the 1% and in favour of working people and the ecosystem that sustains life.

The Green New Deal is a demand for a revolution in international financial relationships, in the globalised economy, and in humanity's relationship to nature. We demand an end to the imperialism of the dollar. An end to the toxic ideology and institutions of capitalism, based on extreme individualism, greed, consumption and competition – and fuelled by spiralling levels of unregulated credit. Instead we insist and will uphold the boundaries and limits imposed by the capacities of both the ecosystem and the economy. We regard it as an urgent priority that the top 20 per cent of the world's big emitters, responsible for 70 per cent of global emissions, are made to radically reduce their carbon use. Carbon equity – between North and South, taking existing stocks of carbon into account – is fundamental to the Green New Deal. Finally, we demand – and will build – an economy based on social and economic justice, one that celebrates the altruism, cooperation and collective responsibility that is a characteristic of human nature.

The Green New Deal can mobilise the efforts of millions of people standing up to the threat of earth systems breakdown, financial sector failure and globalised economic inequality and insecurity. Beneath its canopy we hope to unite and inspire vast numbers of activists across the world and in turn to trigger state action to subordinate finance to the interests of society and the ecosystem – thereby ensuring a liveable planet for people alive today and for future generations. All the while, we should not forget – where there is no struggle, there is no progress.

Acknowledgements

First my warmest thanks to Colin Hines – convenor of the groundbreaking Green New Deal group – for including me in the distinguished circle he gathered around himself over 2007–8, and since then. Thanks are also due to my fellow members – Andrew Simms, Caroline Lucas, Geoff Tily, Charles Secrett, Richard Murphy, Larry Elliott, Jeremy Leggett and Tony Juniper – all esteemed in their fields of endeavour, and from whom I learnt a great deal. We mourn one member of the group, Susie Parsons, who brought good food, laughter and wise counsel to some of our more tempestuous meetings. Due to Colin's radical foresight, his taste for fine white wine, and his warm and generous good humour, we held together despite many hours of lively argument and rigorous debate.

Back in 2000 I was invited to address a fringe meeting at

a conference of heterodox economists on the question of sovereign debt and the international financial system. Three (or was it four?) economists turned up to listen. I complained bitterly that economists, even progressive economists, seemed to ignore the financial system – money, banking, and debt – in their models and in their writings. My audience appeared unmoved. A couple of weeks later a letter arrived from a Dr Geoff Tily, who had been present and agreed with me. Since then Geoff has become a mentor and friend, and has helped deepen my understanding of the international monetary system and of Keynes's monetary theory and policies. I am deeply indebted to him.

Thanks are also due to Leo Hollis of Verso, who urged me to write this book. His support and enthusiasm for my work is what kept me going as I grappled and tried to do justice to the huge issues covered in this modest book. Thanks are also due to Mark Martin and Lorna Fox Scott for fine editing.

Finally, I thank my family – my partner and best friend, Jeremy Smith; my son, Thomas, and his partner Tara Carey – for their patience and much valued support during the writing of this book.

Notes

Preface

1   George Monbiot, 'The Earth Is in a Death Spiral. It Will Take Radical Action to Save Us', *Guardian*, 14 November 2018, theguardian.com, accessed 13 April 2019.

2   Jason Hickel, 'The Hope at the Heart of the Apocalyptic Climate Change Report', *Foreign Policy*, 18 October 2018, foreignpolicy.com, accessed 13 April 2019.

3   Jason W. Moore, 'Slaveship Earth and the World-Historical Imagination in the Age of Climate Crisis', PEWS NEWS, American Sociological Association, 20 May 2018, accessed 5 April 2019.

4   'Who exactly are the 1%', *Economist*, 21 January 2012, economist.com/united-states, accessed 13 April 2019.

5   E. F. Schumacher, *Small Is Beautiful*, Sphere Books, 1974.

6   Monbiot, 'The Earth Is in a Death Spiral'.

7   Kevin Anderson, 'The Hidden Agenda: How Veiled Techno-Utopias Shore Up the Paris Agreement'. A pre-editing and more complete version of a summary of the Paris Agreement published in *Nature's World View*, December 2015, kevinanderson.info, accessed 13 April 2019.

8   Greta Thunberg, "'You did not act in time": Greta Thunberg's Full speech to MPs', *Guardian*, 23 April 2019, theguardian.com, accessed 16 July 2019.

Introduction: What Is the Green New Deal?

1   Thomas L. Friedman, 'A Warning from the Garden', *New York Times*, 19 January 2007, nytimes.com, accessed 19 April 2019.

2   Because of the nature of his employment by the British Treasury, Dr Geoff Tily was not named as a co-author on publication of the Green New Deal report.

3   See Fiona Harvey, 'The Green New Deal: A Massive Injection of Clean Energy Cash', *Financial Times*, 13 March 2009, ft.com, accessed 19 April 2019.

4   Nancy Pelosi quoted on Politico website, 'The Impossible Green Dream of Alexandria Ocasio-Cortez', 7 February 2019, politico.com, accessed 18 April 2019.

5   Abel Gustafson et al., 'The Green New Deal has Strong Bipartisan Support', Yale Program on Climate Change Communication, 14 December 2018, climatecommunication.yale.edu, accessed 15 April 2019.

6   Sean McElwee and John Ray, 'Young People Really, Really Want a Green New Deal', *Nation*, 7 February 2019, thenation.com, accessed 15 April 2019.

7   David Roberts, 'The Green New Deal, explained', *Vox*, 30 March 2019, vox.com, accessed 15 April 2019.

8   116th Congress, 1st Session, 'Resolution Recognizing the Duty of the Federal Government to Create a Green New Deal', 5 February, 2019, assets.documentcloud.org, accessed 16 April 2019.

9   Hannah Northey, 'Meet the Scholar Crafting the "Green New Deal"', E&E News, 27 November 2018, eenews.net/stories, accessed 16 April 2019.

10   Colin Hines et al., 'A Green New Deal: Joined-up Policies to Solve the Triple Crunch of the Credit Crisis, Climate Change and High Oil Prices', New Economics Foundation, 20 July 2008, neweconomics.org, accessed 18 April 2019.

11   Mariana Mazzucato, *The Entrepreneurial State: Debunking Public vs. Private Sector Myths*, Penguin, 2018.

12   Bill McKibben, 'Green New Deal Is a Chance to "Remake Not Just a

Broken Planet, But a Broken Society"', Democracy Now, 15 April 2019, democracynow.org, accessed 18 April 2019.

13   For more on 'the 'Southern Cage' of The New Deal, see Ira Katznelson, *Fear Itself: The New Deal and the Origins of Our Time*, Liveright Publishing Corporation, 2013.

1. System Change, Not Climate Change

1   Simon Pirani, *Burning Up: A Global History of Fossil Fuel Consumption*, Pluto Press, 2018, p. 181.

2   UN Intergovernmental Science-Policy Platform on Biodiversity and Ecosystem Services (IPBES), 6 May 2019, Media Release, ipbes.net, accessed 17 May 2019.

3   Report from the Intergovernmental Science-Policy Platform on Biodiversity and Ecosystem Services (IPBES), 6 May 2019, un.org. sustainabledevelopment/blog, accessed 12 May 2019.

4   Joshua C. Farley, 'The Foundations for an Ecological Economy: An Overview', in Joshua Farley and Deepak Malghan, eds, *Beyond Uneconomic Growth, Vol. 2. A Festschrift in Honor of Herman Daly*, uvm. edu, accessed 29 April 2019.

5   Contraction and Convergence (C&C), Climate Truth and Reconciliation, gci.org.uk, accessed 2 June 2019.

6   Frances Coppola, 'The Myth of Monetary Sovereignty', Brave New Europe, 4 November 2018, braveneweurope.com, accessed 16 June 2019.

7   Adam Tooze, 'Is This the End of the American Century?' *London Review of Books*, 41 (7), 4 April 2019.

8   Pirani, *Burning Up*, p. 194.

9   Ibid.

10   UNODC, *World Drug Report 2018. Global Overview of Drug Demand and Supply*, unodc.org.

11   J. K. Galbraith, quoted in Pirani, *Burning Up*, p. 176.

12   David Roberts, 'This Is an Emergency, Damn It. Green New Deal critics are Missing the Big Picture', *Vox*, 23 February 2019, vox.com, accessed 13 May 2019.

13   Rana Foroohar, *Makers and Takers: The Rise of Finance and the Fall of American Business*, Crown Business Books, 2016, p. 25.

2. Winning the Struggle with Finance

1   Karl Polanyi, *The Present Age of Transformation: Five Lectures*, Policy Research in Macroeconomics (PRIME), 1940, static1.squarespace.com, accessed 13 May 2019.

2   Mark Skousen, *The Making of Modern Economics*, Routledge, 2001, p. 93.

3   Fred Block, introduction to Karl Polanyi, *The Great Transformation*, Beacon Press, 2001, p. 15.

4   Quinn Slobodian, *Globalists: The End of Empire and the Birth of Neoliberalism*, Harvard University Press, 2018, p. 15.

5   Slobodian, *Globalists*.

6   Charles Goodhart, 'The Two Concepts of Money: Implications for the Analysis of Optimal Currency Areas', *European Journal of Political Economy*, 14 (3), 1998: 407–32.

7   Polanyi, *The Present Age of Transformation*, Lecture Two.

8   Edward M. Lamont, *Ambassador from Wall St: The Story of Thomas W. Lamont, J. P. Morgan's Chief Executive*, Madison Books, 1993.

9   Eric Rauchway, *The Money Makers: How Roosevelt and Keynes Ended the Depression, Defeated Fascism, and Secured a Prosperous Peace*, Basic Books, 2015, p. 15.

10 William E. Leuchtenburg, *Franklin D. Roosevelt and the New Deal*, Harper and Row, 1963, p. 8.

11 Rauchway, The Money Makers, p. xxx.

12 Ibid.

13 Geoff Tily, *A Note on the Economic Impact of Roosevelt's New Deal*, TUC's Touchstone blog, 6 April, 2017, touchstoneblog.org.uk.

14 Neil M. Maher, *Nature's New Deal: The Civilian Conservation Corps and the Roots of the American Environmental Movement*, Oxford University Press, 2008, pp. 22.

15 Ibid., pp. 34, 39.

16 Ibid., p. 43.

17 *Civilian Conservation Corps* (CCC), The Living New Deal website, 1933, livingnewdeal.org/glossary, accessed 24 April 2019.

18 Katznelson, *Fear Itself*, p. 176.

19 Maher, *Nature's New Deal*, p. 82.

20   Eric Helleiner, *Forgotten Foundations of Bretton Woods: International Development and the Making of the Postwar Order*, Cornell University Press, 2014.

21   Vishwas Satgar: 'The Question of Our Time: Ending the Capitalist War Against Nature Begins with Eco-socialist Perspectives and Actions', 14 May 2019, africasacountry.com, accessed 17 May 2019.

22   Michael Hudson, '"Creating Wealth" through Debt: The West's Finance–Capitalist Road', Peking University, School of Marxist Studies, 5–6 May 2018, michael-hudson.com.

3. Global System Change

1   See Nassim Nicholas Taleb, *The Black Swan: The Impact of the Highly Improbable*, Penguin, 2008.

2   For more on a Steady State Economy, see Herman E. Daly [1977], *Steady-State Economics* (2nd ed.), Washington, DC, Island Press, 1991.

3   George Monbiot, *Out of the Wreckage*, Verso, 2018.

4   Joshua C. Farley, 'The Foundations for an Ecological Economy: An Overview', in Joshua Farley and Deepak Malghan, eds, *Beyond Uneconomic Growth, Vol. 2. A Festschrift in honor of Herman Daly*, 2018, uvm.edu, accessed 29 April 2019.

5   Herman E. Daly, 'Globalisation and its Inconsistencies', in Ann Pettifor, ed., *Real World Economic Outlook: The Legacy of Globalisation: Debt and Deflation*, New Economics Foundation and Palgrave Macmillan, 2003.

6   Multinational Monitor, 'An Interview with William Brittain-Catlin', August 2005. Offshore: 'Tax Havens, Secrecy, Financial Manipulation, and the Offshore Economy', multinationalmonitor.org, accessed 4 June 2019.

7   Meadows, 'Leverage Points', p. 1.

8   Ibid., p. 17.

9   In 2017 investigative journalists released the Paradise Papers – a trove of 13.4 million records that exposed ties between Russia and US President Donald Trump's billionaire commerce secretary, the secret dealings of the chief fundraiser for Canadian Prime Minister Justin Trudeau, and the offshore interests of the queen of England and more than 120 politicians around the world.

10   Meadows, 'Leverage Points', p. 18, emphasis added.

11   John Maynard Keynes, 'National Self-Sufficiency', *The Yale Review*, 22
     (4), June 1933: 755–69, emphasis added.

12   Colin Hines, *Localization: A Global Manifesto*, Routledge, 2000.

13   See 'Slow Food', wikipedia.org.

14   Global Justice Now Policy Briefing, 'Silent but Deadly: Estimating the
     Real Climate Impact of Agribusiness Corporations', December 2015,
     globaljustice.org.uk.

15   Ian Fitzpatrick, 'Agroecology, not Agribusiness, the Solution to Africa's
     Food Issues Says New Report', 5 March 2015, globaljustice.org.uk,
     accessed 21 May 2019.

16   Global Justice Now, 'Dangerous Delusions', globaljustice.org.uk,
     accessed 21 May 2019.

17   Meadows, 'Leverage Points'.

18   I am grateful to William Brittain-Catlin, author of *Offshore: The Dark
     Side of the Global Economy* (Picador, 2006) for his development of this
     framing. See his article in the *Guardian*, 'Creating an Onshore Nation is
     the Only Way to Restore Financial Sovereignty', 28 December 2010,
     theguardian.com/commentisfree.

19   Ibid.

20   Jagdish Baghwati, 'The Capital Myth: The Difference Between Trade
     in Widgets and Dollars', *Foreign Affairs*, May/June 1998. Available
     from academiccommons.columbia.edu, accessed 22 May 2019.

21   Robert Skidelsky, 'The Great British Laundering Machine', BBC Radio
     4, *File on 4*, 6 February 2018.

22   For a good discussion of current debates on management of capital
     mobility, see Kevin P. Gallagher and Leonardo E. Stanley, 'Capital
     Account Regulations and the Trading System: A Compatibility
     Review', Boston University Frederick S. Pardee Center, 2013,
     networkideas.org, accessed 22 May 2019.

23   See the Federal Reserve's Electronic Code of Federal Regulations, Part
     208 – Membership of State Banking Institutions in the Federal Reserve
     System, ecfr.gov.

24   Daniela Gabor and Cornel Ban, *Banking on Bonds: The New Links
     Between States and Markets*, UWE Bristol and Boston University,
     2015.

25   Akira Ariyoshi et al., 'Capital Controls: Country Experiences with

Their Use and Liberalization', 17 May 2000, imf.org, accessed 24 May 2019.

26   Frances Coppola, 'How China's Capital Controls Help Manage its Foreign Exchange Rate', American Express, n/d, americanexpress. com, accessed 24 May 2019.

4. The Green New Deal Economy

1   For more on the nine planetary boundaries, see the Stockholm Resilience Centre, Stockholm University, stockholmresilience.org.

2   Daly, *Steady-State Economics*, p. 15.

3   Ibid., p. 14.

4   Ibid., p. 17.

5   Ian Gough, *Heat, Greed and Human Need: Climate Change, Capitalism and Sustainable Wellbeing*, Elgar, 2017, p. 42.

6   Ibid., p. 38.

7   Ibid., p. 43.

8   George Monbiot, 'Public Luxury for All or Private Luxury for Some: This Is the Choice We Face', *Guardian*, 31 May 2017, *theguardian.com/ commentisfree*, accessed 1 June 2019.

9   Leigh Phillips and Michal Rozworski, *The People's Republic of Walmart: How the World's Biggest Corporations Are Laying the Foundation for Socialism*, Verso, 2019, p. 236.

10   Friedrich-Ebert-Stiftung Foundation and PSI, full report by Anna Coote and Edanur Yazici, 'Universal Basic Income: A Union Perspective', New Economics Foundation, April 2019, neweconomics. org, accessed 9 June 2019.

11   Nathan Heller, 'Who Really Stands to Win from Universal Basic Income?,' *New Yorker*, 2 July 2018.

12   Anna Coote, 'Are Universal Public Services the Answer to Europe's Widening Inequalities?' Brave New Europe, 4 December 2017, brave-neweurope.com.

13   John Maynard Keynes, CW 21, 'Can America Spend Its Way into Recovery?' First printed in Redbook, December 1934. Reproduced in Robert Skidelsky, *The Essential Keynes*, Penguin, 2015, p. 385.

14   Professor Kevin Anderson, Oxford Climate Society presentation, 24

January 2019, youtube.com/watch?v=7BZFvc-ZOa8&app=desktop, accessed 26 June 2019.

15   Geoff Tily, 'On Prosperity, Growth and Finance', Policy Research in Macroeconomics (PRIME), March 2015, p. 10, static1.squarespace. com, accessed 29 May 2019.

16   Herman E. Daly, *Beyond Growth: The Economics of Sustainable Development*, Beacon Press, 1996, p. 3.

17   Ibid.

18   David Pilling, *The Growth Delusion*, Bloomsbury Publishing, 2018, p. 15.

19   Quoted by Tim Jackson in his essay, 'Everything, in Short, Except That Which Makes Life Worthwhile', 18 March 2018, cusp.ac.uk, accessed 29 May 2019.

20   Tily, 'On Prosperity, Growth and Finance'.

21   Daly, *Beyond Growth*, p. 34.

22   George Lakoff, Daily Archives, #ProtectTheTruth, 18 February 2017, georgelakoff.com, accessed 29 May 2019.

23   Daly, *Beyond Growth*, p. 50.

24   'The Dirty Industry of Fast Fashion', Quartz, 6 March 2018, qz.com, accessed 29 May 2019.

25   Ellen MacArthur Foundation on the Circular Economy, ellenmacarthurfoundation.org.

26   John Vidal, 'Scientists Reveal Fair System for Countries to Tackle Climate Change', *Guardian*, 21 September 2014, theguardian.com/ global development. Stockholm Environment Institute, 'Climate Fairshares', climatefairshares.org/methodology.

5. A Steady State Economy

1   For more on the flaws in William Nordhaus's economics and models, see Aubrey Meyer, *Contraction and Convergence: The Global Solution to Climate Change*, Schumacher Briefings no. 5, Green Books, 2000, p. 51. Also Steve Keen, 'Nordhaus's Nobel Prize Is Safe, but the World Isn't', Patreon, 30 May 2019 (to be published in MINT magazine in July 2019).

2   Douglas Holtz-Eakin, Dan Bosch, Ben Gitis, Dan Goldbeck and Philip Rossetti, 'The Green New Deal: Scope, Scale and Implications',

American Action Forum, 25 February 2019, americanactionforum.org/research, accessed 2 June 2019.

3   Yeva Nersisyan and L. Randall Wray, 'How to Pay for the Green New Deal', Working Paper No. 931, Levy Economics Institute of Bard College, May 2019, levyinstitute.org, accessed 2 June 2019.

4   Hazel Healey, 'What if . . . We Reduced Carbon Emissions to Zero by 2025?,' *New Internationalist*, 6 February 2019.

5   Ibid.

6   Ann Pettifor, *The Production of Money*, Verso, 2017, p. 34.

7   Ann Pettifor, 'International Coordination Saved the Finance Sector, but Not the World', primeeconomics.org/articles, accessed 9 June 2019.

8   Rana Foroohar, *Makers and Takers: The Rise of Finance and the Fall of American Business*, Crown Business, 2016, p. 45.

9   Herman Daly, ed., *Economics, Ecology, Ethics: Essays Toward a Steady-State Economy*, W. H. Freeman and Co., 1973, 1980.

10 Lucas Chancel and Thomas Piketty, 'Carbon and Inequality: From Kyoto to Paris. Trends in the Global Inequality of Carbon Emissions (1998–2013) and Prospects for an Equitable Adaptation Fund', Paris School of Economics, 3 November 2015, p. 31, piketty.pse.ens.fr, accessed 4 June 2019.

11 Kevin Anderson, 'A Succinct Account of My View on Individual and Collective Action', 24 August 2016, kevinanderson.info, accessed 4 June 2019.

12 David Cameron, 'The Age of Austerity', Conservative Party Speech, 26 April 2009, conservative-speeches.sayit.mysociety.org, accessed 4 June 2019.

13 Financial Stability Board, 4 February 2019, pp. 7, 13, and *Global Monitoring Report on Non-Bank Financial Intermediation*, 2018, fsb.org, accessed 30 May 2019.

14 OECD, 'Pension Markets in Focus', 2018, oecd.org.

15 World Bank GDP (Current), data.worldbank.org.

16 Kevin Anderson, 'Trump – The Climate's Secret Champion?,' Infoblog, December, 2018, kevinanderson.info, accessed 26 June, 2019.

17 IMF, 'World Economic Outlook', October 2014, Chapter 3: 'Is It Time for an Infrastructure Push?', imf.org, accessed 3 June 2019. Also Global Commission on the Economy and Climate Report, 2016, 'The Sustainable Infrastructure Imperative: Financing for Better Growth

and Development', newclimateeconomy.report/2016, accessed 3 June 2019.

18   Ibid.

19   'The Costs of Climate Inaction', Editorial, *Nature*, 25 September 2018, nature.com, accessed 30 May 2019.

20   Global Commission on the Economy and Climate Report, 2018, p. 12, newclimateeconomy.report/2018, accessed 30 May 2019.

21   Michael Holder, 'Extreme Weather Costs Global Economy $215bn in 2018, AON Estimates', Business Green, 22 January 2019, business-green.com, accessed 30 May 2019.

22   IMF Working Paper, 'Global Fossil Fuel Subsidies Remain Large: An Update Based on Country-Level Estimates', 2 May 2019, imf.org.

23   Global Commission on the Economy and Climate Report, 2018, p. 14.

24   Climate Disclosure Project, 'The Carbon Majors Database. CDP Carbon Majors Report 2017', rackcdn.com/cms/reports, accessed 5 June 2019.

25   Nicole Badstuber, 'London Congestion Charge Has Been a Huge Success. It's Time to Change It', City Metric, *New Statesman*, 12 March 2018, citymetric.com.

6. The Green New Deal: Transforming Our World

1   Mariana Mazzucato, *The Entrepreneurial State: Debunking Public vs. Private Sector Myths*, Anthem Press, 2013.

2   Daniela Gabor and Cornel Ban, 'Banking on Bonds: The New Links between States and Markets', 2015, bu.edu/pardeeschool.

3   Manmohan Singh, 'Collateral Reuse and Balance Sheet Space', IMF Working Paper, Washington, DC, 2017, imf.org.

4   Wanda Vrasti, 'This Courage Called Utopia', The Disorder of Things, 9 November 2012, thedisorderofthings.com, accessed 12 June 2019.

5   Andrew Simms and Peter Newell, Rapid Transition Alliance, 'Evidence-Based Hope', rapidtransition.org, accessed 12 June 2019.

6   Ibid.

7   Andrew Simms and Peter Newell, *How Did We Do That? The Possibility of Rapid Transition*, STEPS Centre and the New Weather Institute pamphlet, 2018, p. 12, newweather.org, accessed 12 June 2019.

8   Ibid., p. 23.

9   Louis Hyman, 'The New Deal Wasn't What You Think', *Atlantic*, 6 March 2019, theatlantic.com.

10 Ibid.

11 Ben Quinn, 'Gordon Brown: Unity of UK at Risk from "Hijacking of Patriotism', *Guardian*, 25 June 2019, theguardian.com.

12 Biography of Wangari Maathai, Green Belt Movement, greenbelt-movement.org, accessed 17 June 2019.

13 Franck Prévot, illustrated by Aurélia Fronty, *Wangari Maathai: The Woman Who Planted Millions of Trees*, Charlesbridge, 2017, charles-bridge.com, accessed 17 June 2019.

14 Frederick Douglass, 'If There Is No Struggle, There Is No Progress', 1857 speech, blackpast.org, accessed 17 June 2019.